riding in the
Z◯NE

advanced techniques for skillful motorcycling

ken condon

Whitehorse Press
Center Conway, New Hampshire

With a few exceptions, photographs were taken by the author. Special thanks to photographer, John Owens Photography for his wonderful action photos on the cover (main image) and on pages 1, 5, 6, 7, 92, 108, and 140 (lower) taken during race events and at the track days. www.owensracingphotos.com

Thanks to other photo contributors for sharing their work: Jeannine Condon 28 (lower image), 30, 34, 41, 44 (lower image), 58 (middle image), 141; Tony Iannarelli 29 (lower image); Ken Mitchell 22 (bottom image), 56, 112; Tim Moore 23 (upper image), Tim Richer 64, and Caroline White 70, 29 (upper image), 128 (upper image), 135 (upper image).

We recognize that some words, model names, and designations mentioned herein are the property of the trademark holder. We use them for identification purposes only.

Whitehorse Press books are also available at discounts in bulk quantity for sales and promotional use. For details about special sales or for a catalog of Whitehorse Press motorcycling books, write to the publisher:

Whitehorse Press
107 East Conway Road
Center Conway, New Hampshire 03813
Phone: 603-356-6556 or 800-531-1133
E-mail: CustomerService@WhitehorsePress.com
Internet: www.WhitehorsePress.com

ISBN: 978-1-884313-76-9

5 4 3 2

Printed in China

WARNING: Riding motorcycles is inherently dangerous and can result in serious injury or death. We believe the information in this book and video to be accurate to the best of the author's and the publisher's knowledge; however, you should be aware that there are many differing opinions about riding technique and concepts. The recommendations contained in this book and video are made without any guarantee on the part of the author or publisher, who also disclaim any liability incurred in connection with the use of these recommendations.

Drills described and shown in the video are performed by an expert rider and are included for demonstration purposes only. Do not perform the drills yourself if you are unsure of your ability to do so safely. Always ride within your personal limits and always wear protective gear.

foreword

I'm not a gambling man, but I've noticed that a lot of great things get started by chance. I met Ken Condon in 1999 at the Americade rally at Lake George, NY where Ken's wife was working. Ken apparently recognized me from my image and wandered over. "Hey, aren't you the guy who writes for MCN?" It wasn't long into our natter before Ken asked me how he might break into the motorcycle journalism field. As it happened, I was approaching age 65 and was worn out after 30 years of generating monthly skills columns.

Ken seemed to be genuinely interested, and he had the right stuff. He was an experienced street and dirt rider, an amateur road racer, and a certified instructor. He was a professional illustrator and photographer. He just needed to learn how to write, so I offered to help.

That summer I bumped into Ken again, during a motorcycle safety conference in Milwaukee. Harley-Davidson had invited everyone to come out to the engine plant, with free hot dogs and a Buell "Battletrax" course set up in the parking lot. I tippy-toed a Buell around the course somewhere slower than 50 seconds. Ken made his first pass just under 40 seconds, and after a few runs had whittled his time down to under 30 seconds.

That was the first time I saw Ken ride a bike, and frankly, I was impressed. Afterward, Ken cornered me and asked again about writing. I asked if he was serious. Yes, he'd been thinking it over, and he wanted to do it.

Prior to the 2000 Americade I flew to the right coast and rode down to Massachusetts to spend some time with Ken. We exchanged ideas, and by the next spring we were ready to propose a new Proficient Motorcycling contributor to MCN editor, Dave Searle.

That got Ken's foot in the door at MCN. At first, I would continue to generate columns, alternating with Ken's columns. The transition appeared seamless, which in my mind meant easing slowly away from the "Hough" style MCN readers had come to expect.

By the following year Ken was generating all of the Proficient Motorcycling articles for MCN. After a while he also took over writing the Street Strategies column.

While I was pleased that Ken was filling the monthly squares for MCN, I was eager to see what would happen when he "found his own voice." When I heard that Ken was writing his own book, I realized that he had *arrived*. I'm pleased to have been his mentor, giving back to the sport the same way my mentors Bob Carpenter and Fred Rau helped me along. It was a good gamble.

I knew you could achieve great things, Ken. *Riding in the Zone* is proof of that.

David L. Hough, author of Proficient Motorcycling

There is little that can match the sublime sensation of rolling down a peaceful road, or the invigorating feeling that comes from slicing skillfully through a series of challenging corners. These moments are what riding is all about. However, for a lot of riders not every trip is so enjoyable.

Every motorcycle rider I know experiences some aspect of riding that causes anxiety, whether it's negotiating traffic, handling complex corners, or maneuvering in tight spaces. A short-term solution to these difficult situations is to simply avoid them, but wouldn't it be better to learn how to deal with them? By learning how to manage the riding environment expertly and control their motorcycle with precision, motorcyclists can replace anxiety with confidence.

about the author

With more than three decades of motorcycle riding experience, including road racing, touring, dirt riding, and commuting I have learned what it takes to become a skillful, confident rider.

During the past dozen years I have acted as a Motorcycle Safety Foundation (MSF) instructor and as a track day instructor coaching all types of riders, ranging from raw beginners to accomplished veterans. I've also been a part of the burgeoning motorcycle careers both of my wife Caroline and daughter Jeannine who are now both proficient riders.

In addition to my experience as an instructor I am the author of the monthly Proficient Motorcycling and Street Strategies columns for *Motorcycle Consumer News*.

My experience as a riding coach and author has taught me how to recognize problems and communicate solutions to help riders become more skillful and confident. In that spirit, I hope this book will help you, too. Visit me at www.RidingInTheZone.com.

who this book is for

Riding in the Zone is written for the early-intermediate to early-advanced motorcycle rider who has a desire to ride with greater confidence. This includes newer riders with a solid understanding of basic motorcycle control as well as veteran motorcyclists who seek increased riding mastery and enjoyment.

Riding in the Zone explores both the mental and physical aspects of motorcycling. You'll learn new ways to manage risk and discover how to adopt a confidence-inspiring attitude.

Riding in the Zone also explains and illustrates riding techniques that I have carefully chosen to target the most common trouble spots. Some of these riding skills and techniques are included simply because they are so essential to a solid riding foundation. Other more advanced techniques are included to help you refine motorcycle control and increase confidence.

using the book and video

Riding in the Zone is divided into three parts. **Part I – The Confident Rider,** describes the characteristics of confidence and how to increase it. You'll also learn to recognize factors that conspire to diminish riding confidence and enjoyment.

Part II - Mental Skill Development – Taking Command of the Environment, introduces you to risk-reducing strategies, the importance of highly attuned visual acuity, and ways to develop a traction "sense." Each of these topics aims to enhance your connection with your motorcycle and surroundings.

Part III - Physical Skill Development – Mastering Motorcycle Control, presents specific techniques to help you maintain maximum control when braking, cornering, and shifting, as well as body positioning for increased bike/rider interaction and control.

Drills are included at the end of each chapter to help you transform ideas and concepts into solid skills.

A companion DVD that explains and demonstrates most of the concepts and techniques discussed in the book is included to help you apply its lessons to actual street riding. The video is not a replacement for the book; rather, it is a supplement that will enable you to better understand and visualize each concept and technique.

You can read and refer to the information in this book and DVD in any order you prefer. Read, watch, and practice so the skills become second nature.

References to the video segments are located on pages where topics are discussed.

Look for this symbol:

the confident rider

Part I explores the psychology of riding with confidence. You'll learn what factors increase confidence and recognize conditions that threaten riding confidence, so you can minimize their effect. Part I also discusses your relationship with risk and takes a comprehensive look at the risks we face as motorcyclists.

In this chapter, you will learn to identify the specific characteristics of confidence and evaluate current attitudes and behaviors that may be eroding your confidence and holding you back from experiencing maximum enjoyment and satisfaction from each ride.

confidence defined

Confidence is an aspect of human experience that is not measurable, yet it is as real as any material object. Confidence is a feeling of trust in yourself and your abilities. It is a sense of well-being driven by reasonable certainty that you will be able to handle whatever is thrown your way.

Confidence is a very personal thing. Some people are confident at some things and quite terrified at the thought of others. A motorcycle rider who is adept at all aspects of motorcycle control has the potential to make each ride a joyful experience, whereas people who are less proficient can easily become discouraged when facing challenges that are beyond their comfort zone.

A high level of confidence makes riding more enjoyable, and it also frees your mind of anxious distractions so you can more easily pick up subtle environmental and visceral information. With your mind unencumbered with stress you can predict outcomes before they occur and sense subtle stimuli that you couldn't otherwise. The result is a sense of security and mastery that translates to a truly enjoyable and satisfying ride.

Not only does a high confidence level increase your likelihood for a deeper riding experience, it can also encourage you to try new things. With a strong sense of self-assurance you are more likely to engage in new adventures and challenge yourself to grow.

the zone reward

When you are confident you feel self-assured, competent, and comfortable. This happy condition makes for a good time, but it can lead to much more: a deeper connection between you, your motorcycle, and your surroundings. Some people call this being "in the groove" or "in the zone."

Riding in the zone is an extraordinary state of being when your mind is in sync with the environment, and your muscles interact harmoniously with your motorcycle—you are "one" with your motorcycle and the road. You know you're in the zone when you are fully immersed in the experience and your attention is pinpoint-focused.

Being in the zone can feel as though your ride has become an active meditation; life's problems go silent and every thought you have is transfixed in the present moment. The linear framework of seconds and minutes typical of daily life ceases to exist. Once you have experienced the zone it becomes a goal to strive for—and the more aware and open you are to the zone, the more likely you are to experience it.

accessing the zone

The zone is accessible any time you swing your leg over a motorcycle. However, accessing the zone can be elusive because the zone is a state of being that materializes only when conditions are right—conditions over which we have only partial control. Even though the zone can be difficult to conjure, the probability of a zone experience is greatly increased when you feel composed and confident.

People experience enjoyment in different ways, but we all experience the most joy when we feel competent and are reasonably certain that our well-being is secure; otherwise anxiety takes over and happiness fades. Much of our confidence in riding motorcycles comes from having highly developed skills. A rider with a high level of competence believes that he or she can handle most, if not all, situations; this confidence is the bridge to zone experiences. In contrast, riders who lack the skills that promote confidence tend to feel on edge and unprepared for the unexpected—not exactly an enjoyable condition.

A prerequisite for experiencing the zone is an absolute focus in the present moment. However, "being in the moment" requires discipline to prevent your mind's incessant chatter from disrupting the interplay between you, your motorcycle, and the road. Achieving total focus is easy when facing a challenging task that requires your full concentration, but zone moments can occur just as easily when riding at a relaxed pace on a beautifully scenic road. It's even possible to experience the zone when riding in traffic. It matters less where you ride than it does how confident you are in your abilities and whether your attention is fully focused in the moment.

false confidence

Many motorcyclists feel little anxiety while riding. This enhances enjoyment, but their sense of confidence may be based on a self-assessment that is dangerously unrealistic.

Confidence isn't always an accurate gauge of a rider's capabilities. Some riders achieve a state of confidence through a naïve "come what may" attitude while others base their confidence on an inflated ego, an over-optimistic attitude, or inexperience. Any one of these conditions can easily lull people into thinking they are more capable than they are. Confidence built on abilities that may not exist leaves you more vulnerable to hazards.

Confidence can also be derived from other false sources, the most dangerous being alcohol. One characteristic of intoxication is an inflated sense of self-assurance and mastery, which often leads to poor judgement and disastrous outcomes.

Be aware that your sense of confidence may not be accurate. Evaluate whether your sense of confidence is based on a strong foundation of skill, or on fantasy. It's great to feel confident, but not in defiance of common sense and safety.

Whether you're a beginner or an expert rider, there is great satisfaction in skill development.

building skills and confidence

While it may be true that experience alone can teach you what you need to know to become a skillful, confident rider, these lessons often come at a high cost. The best way to become more proficient without attending the School of Hard Knocks is to actively develop skills before you need them.

The skills that confident motorcyclists acquire include keen risk awareness and risk management, along with the ability to handle a motorcycle masterfully. Motorcycle riders possess varying degrees of these traits; they are usually confident at some tasks and anxious about others. If you pay attention you will likely recognize situations when your confidence level isn't as high as it could be.

To enjoy motorcycling to its fullest you must recognize the areas where you can improve and develop your skills, so that confidence, not anxiety, governs your riding experience.

mental development

Confident riders possess strong mental skills together with excellent physical skills. It's this combination that nurtures confidence and makes riding a motorcycle safe and fun.

Unfortunately, many people automatically equate riding mastery with the physical ability to handle a motorcycle expertly and don't think much about mental skills. While physical skills *are* critical for safe and enjoyable riding, it's the *mental* skills that carry the most weight in preparing you for problems and instilling confidence.

Superior mental skills minimize the need for superior physical skills. For instance, a missed clue about a left-hand car turning in front of you results in the need for evasive action, whereas sharp skills for detecting such situations lead to less extreme preemptive action and little drama. All the physical ability in the world won't remedy poor judgement or the inability to manage challenging situations. A rider who is very skilled at controlling his or her motorcycle, but chooses to ignore risk, may demonstrate a high level of confidence, but is flirting with trouble.

A truly proficient motorcycle rider may not be the best at tricky maneuvers or the fastest through the curves, but he or she is highly capable at motorcycle control and is smart about how to manage traffic and handle complex cornering situations. This rider will likely experience many safe, enjoyable rides.

↘ the confident mindset

When riding a motorcycle it's important to feel reasonably confident that your safety is assured, otherwise anxiety takes over and happiness fades. A strong sense of confidence begins with well-developed mental skills that include a desire to grow and a healthy respect for the risks of riding.

motivation to learn

You don't have to be an expert to feel confident. As a matter of fact, novice riders experience a sense of confidence as frequently as experts. Watch the first hour of any beginner riding course and you'll see the intense concentration of the students as they simply ride across a parking lot. This focused attention soon turns to joy. Their smiles are fueled by a feeling of accomplishment and the increased sense of confidence that comes from learning how to control a motorcycle within the controlled environment of the training range. Even after they graduate from the parking lot onto the streets, every achievement feels like a victory and confidence continues to grow.

Experienced riders benefit just as much from learning. I've seen many veteran riders express great satisfaction after discovering a new skill, breaking old habits, or refining braking or cornering techniques in an MSF class or on the racetrack.

The long-term reward for improving your riding skills is to achieve better control and reduce risk, but safety alone is not a big motivator for a lot of riders. A more common motivator is the promise that riding can be even more fun and gratifying. The work you do to improve your skills will build upon itself and reward you with greater proficiency and security.

The motivation for growth must come from within you. Peer pressure and other outside influences may offer some superficial incentive, but external motivation won't last. Motivation will come more easily if you keep in mind that the reward for becoming a better rider is greater confidence and more satisfying motorcycling experiences.

challenges

Being suitably challenged contributes significantly to a feeling of satisfaction. Challenges are opportunities for us to become better than we currently are. When we are challenged our mind becomes fully occupied with the task at hand and we are forced to become fully immersed in the ride.

It's important to recognize, however, that biting off too much can cause harmful anxiety. In contrast, a lack of challenge leads to energy-sapping boredom that rarely results in enjoyable riding experiences. Somewhere in the middle is just the right amount of challenge that avoids complacency without causing excessive anxiety.

The thrill of stretching your limits is a significant source of riding enjoyment. The act of trying a new technique or attacking a corner more aggressively increases alertness and adrenaline flow. But, be careful; there is a fine line between stretching your limits and riding beyond your abilities. Finding yourself in a situation you cannot handle prompts feelings of panic and apprehension. This stressful state of anxiety is no fun and can lead to injury. Keep your challenges within reach of your abilities and expect to grow incrementally as your skills and confidence allow.

Develop your "traffic awareness" by pretending you are playing a video game that requires you to spot subtle sounds, movements, and traffic patterns before they manifest into hazardous situations. Some of the "clues" you are presented with by other drivers might include very slight adjustments in speed or a subtle arm movement that hints at a left-hand turn across your lane. You get "points" each time you accurately predict an errant maneuver. Play this mental game on every ride you take. Eventually, you will have a well-developed traffic sense that may save your skin some day. As a bonus, you'll discover that this game makes even mundane rides more fun.

awareness and attention

A sharp state of awareness contributes greatly to a sense of confidence. Important information is available to those who are alert to their surroundings and listen to their intuition. Riders who develop this "sixth sense" are totally involved in the moment and have a keen awareness of their environment. These riders pick up subtle clues and are able to predict traffic behavior much earlier than those who are less in tune.

For instance, a truck approaches in the oncoming lane as you near an intersection. Something tells you that the truck is about to turn left across your path. It may be a barely noticeable change in speed or a subtle body movement from the driver that your brain translates as a sign that something is about to happen. You instinctively respond to the sensation by rolling off the throttle, covering your brakes, and moving to the far side of your lane. Sure enough, the truck slows abruptly and begins to turn, but you're way ahead of the situation and are able to slow in time to avoid a collision.

This sixth sense is also present when no obvious hazards are near. For instance, you might detect tension when negotiating a series of curves. This stress is trying to tell you that you're going a bit too fast for the conditions or your comfort level. Or, a voice inside your helmet whispers that you might want to get ready to stop—just before an animal darts from the roadside brush.

An important aspect of riding with confidence is having the skill to maintain focus and attention so you can sense these sometimes subtle messages. It can be easy to let every-day thoughts and emotions distract you, but you can prevent this from happening with a bit of discipline. Get into the habit of periodically "checking in" with yourself during a ride to ensure that you are concentrating on the task at hand. Staying focused and attentive allows your mind to pick up subtle environmental clues, but it also leads to refined control as your brain works harmoniously with your body to brake, shift, and corner with precision.

sensory development

Another aspect of awareness is developing the ability to sense whether or not you have enough traction to remain in control.

In the vast majority of situations, traction is abundant and an intense level of awareness isn't necessary. However, this feedback becomes very important when you are suddenly facing a tricky maneuver on a questionable surface or when determining whether there is sufficient traction to corner safely.

There is no magic way to develop this sensitivity except by heightening your awareness. Learning this visceral language is a critical step toward achieving a deeper connection to riding. The more fluent you are, the more open the channel of communication between you and your motorcycle.

riding strategies and physical skills

Up until now, I've focused on mental skills that nurture riding enjoyment, but to ride with confidence also requires other resources, such as strategies for staying safe in traffic and excellent physical skills, such as proficient braking and cornering.

I won't go into the details of strategies or physical skills just yet. Those will come in Part II and Part III. For now, let's continue to concentrate on ways you can increase your riding enjoyment.

expand your experiences

It is beneficial to consider various motorcycle activities when you want to expand your experience and introduce new challenges. You may very well discover a new way to enjoy riding or rekindle your passion for motorcycling and increase confidence along the way.

By expanding your riding experiences you introduce opportunities to increase knowledge and growth. These experiences can be intense, such as what racers encounter when ripping around a racetrack, or sublime, a common experience of most street riders as they commute to work or cruise with friends on a Sunday afternoon. One is not better than the other; rather each offers its own unique way for you to learn and grow. Here are a few examples of motorcycling opportunities that you may like to try.

sharing the ride

There's nothing better than sharing the freedom of the road—the thrill of carving corners and the contentment of discovering new places and viewing beautiful scenery—with a passenger or a group of friends. But to share the ride safely requires that your riding skills be excellent; you can't expect those who ride with you to be relaxed and have a good time if you can't handle your motorcycle capably.

You may not have thought about it, but passengers must have confidence too. It takes time and patience for a passenger to become a proficient partner, but a bit of parking lot practice can help ease a new passenger into their new role and make the process very satisfying for both of you. The most challenging part of motorcycling for a passenger is cornering. Tell your passenger to lean with you and the motorcycle. This is easier said than done, but one trick to help them accomplish this is to ask them to look over your shoulder in the direction of the turn. Before you know it you'll hear whoops of joy and requests for future rides.

Group riding is also a great way to expand motorcycling enjoyment. Sharing a ride with a group of like-minded individuals with a similar passion for motorcycling and an appreciation for proficient riding is a recipe for fun. Be careful though: riding in a group can be risky if peer pressure and pack behavior take over. Additionally, you can be negatively affected by riders who are less skilled. Include only smart, skilled motorcyclists in your group rides to maximize enjoyment and minimize risk.

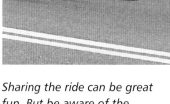

Sharing the ride can be great fun. But be aware of the risks and responsibilities.

↘ on your next ride

It takes a rather high level of awareness to recognize and understand the subtle messages coming from your motorcycle. Pay attention to how your motorcycle responds. Does the motorcycle turn with little effort or do you sense resistance? Does the motorcycle hold its line in corners or does it drift wide? These are two examples of the types of questions astute riders ask themselves to assess cornering problems.

Unpredictable handling or a reluctance of your motorcycle to turn may indicate poor suspension setup or a mechanical problem. It may also indicate a need to relax your arms. Also, a disconnected feeling between the handlebars and the road while braking or cornering may indicate imminent traction loss.

travel

There is a special feeling of camaraderie between you and your motorcycle when you are far from home. There's a sense that your bike is a trustworthy friend who is always ready for another day's adventure and will dutifully return you home at the end of your journey.

Visiting new places exposes you to situations you might not have experienced otherwise. If you haven't ventured more than a day or two away from home, you owe it to yourself to give motorcycle travel a try.

racing

Racing is perhaps the pinnacle of riding prowess. The act of riding very fast amongst other riders who wish to cross the finish line ahead of you requires the utmost skill. Total mental focus and physical precision are prerequisites and there is little room allowed for lapses in concentration or control. It is said that racing improves the breed. If you want the most intense opportunity for growth you can't beat racing.

Of course, racing isn't for everyone. It requires an acceptance of risk that most people will never tolerate. But, before you discount racing, ask whether your street riding might not be more risky. If you tend to ride aggressively on the street, then you may very well be risking more than racers who push the limits in a controlled environment under ideal conditions. If you are unable to ride on the street at a speed that allows generous time and space to respond to typical hazard scenarios, then perhaps it's time to sign up for a race school. If the idea of racing makes you queasy, consider attending a track day. Track days are appropriate for riders of all skill levels, not just those who ride aggressively on the street. (See Chapter 11 for more on track days.)

dirt riding

Dirt riding can be an eye opening experience for a pavement rider. Even simple tasks such as braking and cornering become new challenges because the techniques and terrain differ from the more predictable street riding environment.

There is great satisfaction in navigating through a field of boulders, surmounting fallen trees, or traversing a knee-deep stream. Not only will this venue deliver a new thrill, but your newly acquired skillset will help you develop a keener traction sense that translates well to street riding.

mechanical connection

Another way to gain confidence is to get your hands dirty. Having an intimate understanding of how your motorcycle works can give you the confidence to evaluate mechanical problems, which can come in handy if problems occur on a motorcycle trip far from home.

Every rider should be able to check tire pressures, maintain the drive train, and change oil. Those who are more mechanically inclined might consider taking on more complex tasks, such as upgrading suspension components to improve handling, adjusting valve clearances, replacing brake pads, and repacking bearings. Of course, you must be smart about what you choose to tackle. If in doubt, contact a knowledgeable friend or your local dealer.

The act of maintaining the mechanical integrity and appearance of your motorcycle involves more than turning wrenches and polishing chrome. It's a nurturing act of mechanical appreciation. You'll take new pride in your motorcycle after installing a new chain and sprocket set or adjusting your suspension for a better ride and feel pride in yourself for being able to do it.

By developing your mental and physical skills and finding new ways to expand your motorcycling experiences you will acquire more confidence and enjoy many happy motorcycling miles.

2

Threats that cause anxiety and increase risk conspire to undermine confidence and reduce the likelihood that you will experience the zone. These threats may come from external sources such as poor road conditions and traffic, or internal sources such as a destructive attitude or underdeveloped skills. By evaluating your mental state, recognizing these barriers, and acting to minimize their effect, you are more likely to remain in focus and ride with greater confidence.

This chapter discusses threats, especially the commonly unrecognized attitudes and behaviors that hold riders back from enjoying motorcycling to its fullest.

external threats

Erratic drivers, poorly maintained roads, and traction-robbing surface debris can be a real drag. It is tempting to curse these threats and blame them for your discord, but dwelling on the shortcomings of your riding environment is a waste of time. Instead, you are better served by developing skills to manage these threats successfully.

Even though these threats can reduce the pleasure of a perfect ride, meeting the challenges these external threats present can be quite satisfying—as long as you have developed strategies to deal with them and are adept at responding appropriately. Chapter 4 describes ways to manage many of the risks in this threat category.

Left-turning vehicles are a very common external threat.

internal threats

Internal threats are self-induced behaviors that undermine confidence. These threats include weak strategies for riding safely in traffic, inadequate physical skills, poor judgement, and risky behavior that includes riding while distracted or intoxicated. Riders with weak mental and physical skills experience frequent close calls and anxiety, which can cause their confidence to plummet and enjoyment to wane.

Some riders blame close calls on "the other guy" or the road itself, not understanding or accepting their responsibility to manage the risks. These riders may display their lack of understanding by claiming they had to "lay it down" to avoid a collision or by insisting that "there was nothing they could do" when a car appeared "out of nowhere." The fact is that most mishaps can be avoided with proficient control skills and strategies for predicting hazards.

By adopting an attitude that values less risk, staying focused on the moment, learning to control your motorcycle with precision, and developing traffic management strategies you can minimize the effects of these internal threats and enhance your confidence and enjoyment.

risky behavior

Choosing to take extreme risks by stunting in traffic, street racing, or drinking and riding is the greatest internal threat to confidence—or of long-term survival. Riders who behave in ways that are likely to lead to injury are usually in denial of the real risks of riding a motorcycle, but some riders fully understand the risk yet choose to ride dangerously anyway. While pushing the limits can be invigorating, extreme risk-taking is foolhardy. Such behavior will eventually lead to sorrowful outcomes.

If you discover that you just can't control the urge to ride fast on the street, consider spending more time on the racetrack and less time on the public roads. Track days are offered in many places and are open to a very wide range of street riders. Track days are discussed in greater detail in Chapter 11.

Most importantly, don't drink and ride! Social drinking has been a part of motorcycle culture for many decades and can be incredibly difficult to resist when your riding friends subscribe to this behavior. But, it is imperative that you recognize that riding impaired carries significant risk to yourself and those around you.

peer pressure

Group riding can lead to many enjoyable experiences. But, group riding can also turn scary if normally easygoing individuals succumb to pack behavior with excessive speeds or other anti-social behavior. Individuals disappear into the false protection of the collective whole where inhibitions dissolve and bravado flourishes. It's easy to get caught up in the fervor of a group ride; however this situation often turns stressful and dangerous.

Whether you find yourself on a charity ride or part of an impromptu meeting on the road, recognize the competitive posing that often emerges. Learn to recognize when ego or pride clouds your judgement and resist the urge to keep up with faster riders or show off your superior riding skills to those who might notice. This is a recipe for disaster.

Also, be aware of other behaviors that peers might influence, such as not wearing safety gear because your riding friends don't, or doing stunts in traffic because they do. Recognize when you are being pulled by these pack influences and strengthen your resolve to ride smart.

Sharing the ride can be great fun. But be aware of the risks and responsibilities.

impatience

Annoyance toward slow drivers is common, especially if you are late to your destination or if a driver is interrupting your rhythm through an invigorating series of corners. This state of frustration can ruin your mood and lead to poor decisions. Instead of acting on your impatience, choose to resist tailgating and remain calm until a safe opportunity to pass is available. If no such opportunity is forthcoming, then take a breath and try to accept the situation.

One solution is to pull over to allow the slow car to get ahead. After a few moments you can proceed on your way without the tension and frustration of riding slower than you prefer.

unrealistic expectations

Motorcycle riding stirs images of relaxation, freedom, and enjoyment, but this idealistic expectation isn't always possible. The fact is that some rides are ho-hum. A ride can even turn out to be disappointing if your rhythm is off or you are just not "feeling it."

Another source of angst comes from unrealistic personal expectations. For example, if you seek to become an expert rider in an unrealistically short amount of time, you will likely become discouraged.

Instead, take a step back so you can devote the necessary time and attention it takes to become proficient. Also, it's important to forgive yourself when you make a mistake. Nobody is perfect. Learn from mistakes and use them to focus your skill-building efforts on ways to overcome personal handicaps. And don't neglect to recognize things you do right.

stagnation

Stagnation is another condition that can erode confidence and diminish enjoyment. For instance, riding can grow to be dull if you always ride on the same roads with the same friends on the same motorcycle. The antidote to stagnation is to try new things.

To revive the excitement of riding, consider some of the activities mentioned in the last chapter: take a long trip, attend a track day, or take up dirt riding. Another challenge is to master slow-speed riding. You may scoff at this suggestion, but mastering slow-speed handling is very challenging and satisfying. A Motorcycle Safety Foundation riding course is an excellent place to learn and practice slow-speed maneuvers. Or, you can set up an obstacle course and have a "slow race" with a few friends.

At some point most riders experience a plateau of enthusiasm when there appear to be few new adventures or challenges. Regard this as an indicator that you are ready to move to a higher level of proficiency. Reaching that next stage begins by realizing that there is still opportunity to grow, then deciding which of the many opportunities you'd like to pursue. The pursuit of these opportunities can spark enthusiasm and self-satisfaction and is fertile ground for renewed confidence.

Keep stagnation at bay by expanding your skillset and range of experience.

after a fall

A crash can shatter your confidence and devastate your piece of mind—and the effects can linger for a long time. The good news is that a crash doesn't have to diminish the joy of riding. It depends on how you respond to the trauma. You may be able to soften the psychological blow by pinpointing the internal and external reasons for the crash and making a plan to prevent a similar mishap from happening in the future. This may be easy or difficult, but learning from the incident is your best way to move past it.

It's easy to understand the cause and solution of a lowside fall on a patch of sand while cornering: slow down, use a wide corner entry so you can spot surface hazards earlier, and learn to manage low traction situations more effectively. The following chapters will help you develop these techniques.

A crash involving a second vehicle adds another level of complication, especially if the actions of the other driver appear to have been completely irrational. These crashes are frightful, because we naturally base our decisions on reasonable behavior by other drivers, expecting them to stay in their lane and obey traffic rules.

To benefit most from post-crash analysis, you must suspend blame. Assigning blame to someone else is a natural emotional response, but can blind you from recognizing your part in a close call or crash. A rider who fails to take responsibility for mishaps will not learn from the incident and is very likely to be involved in another similar situation in the future.

You've probably heard other riders tell harrowing stories about their crashes or near crashes, proclaiming how "that SOB just pulled right out in front of me." Yes, other motorists are often to blame in multi-vehicle crashes that involve motorcycles, but most times there was something the rider could have done to help prevent the incident from happening.

↘ learn from experience

Reflect on a recent crash or close call you had involving a vehicle crossing into your right of way. Put yourself in the seat of the driver who invaded your path. What made him or her think it was okay to proceed? It's likely that the driver either didn't see you, or saw you but did not accurately judge your speed and distance.

Help drivers see you by wearing bright clothing and selecting a lane position that increases your conspicuity. You must also slow down around intersecting traffic to give drivers time to notice you and to allow you the time and space you need to take evasive action if necessary. Finally, develop a heightened awareness so you can better predict when a driver may act inappropriately.

fatigue and distraction

Riding a motorcycle requires a sharp mind and sharp senses. Riding when you are fatigued is a sure way to increase risk. It's easy to recognize some forms of fatigue, such as when you have had minimal sleep or when you are exhausted after a hard day at work. But other times, fatigue can sneak up on you as the miles roll by during a long trip.

Fatigue causes your senses to dull and your reaction times to increase. Exhaustion also creates dangerous distraction that can cause you to miss important clues about traffic movement or surface hazards. Be sure to stay on top of your mental and physical condition to head off any significant distraction due to fatigue.

A prerequisite for riding with confidence is being aware of what threatens your well-being and knowing what to do about it. The next chapter covers risk awareness in detail, to help you develop mental and physical skills to manage these threats.

3

Riding a motorcycle requires more than simply being able to operate the controls and stay in balance. It also takes a conscious understanding of the risks and a determination to reduce those risks as much as possible. The probability of zone experiences increases when risk is minimized. Keeping risk within a comfortable range increases confidence and reduces distraction, which frees your mind to observe the nuances of motorcycle feedback and the subtleties of your riding environment.

This chapter explores the nature of risk and the relationship you have with risk. You'll learn how to build your perceptual skills and we will discuss specific high-risk situations to help you be prepared for them when they arise.

risk perception and denial

Ignorance may be bliss, but it can also be hazardous. We'd all like to believe that motorcycling is less risky than it is, but you're much better off accepting that riding is dangerous and work toward developing skills to minimize risk.

The most vulnerable people on two wheels are those who treat risk lightly. These riders are more likely to be caught in situations they are not prepared for; they don't consider the life-threatening situations they might face, because they haven't faced them—yet.

Sometimes, perceptions of risk are based on inaccurate, preconceived notions. For instance, some riders think that riding a motorcycle is similar enough to driving a car that they don't consider the need for specialized information or training. Even though these riders may want to reduce risk as much as possible, they are unknowingly increasing the probability of a mishap through ignorance.

Those who treat risk lightly are at great risk.

To define risk accurately, you must consider three factors: the probability of a mishap, your risk exposure, and the consequences of a particular crash.

The probability of being involved in a crash depends partly on your perception of risk; those who consider riding a motorcycle to be risky will ride more carefully, whereas someone who sees the risk of riding as minimal is more likely to take chances. Your probability of crash involvement also depends upon your riding environment and your risk exposure; riding in heavy traffic exposes you to a greater probability of a collision with another vehicle compared to riding in a remote rural area. The consequence of a particular crash depends largely on the speed at the time of the fall and whether you impact a solid object.

risk profile

Risk means different things to different people; some riders are repulsed by risk and avoid it, others are stimulated by it. Of course most people have a tolerance for risk somewhere between these two extremes. The majority of us ride motorcycles because we enjoy the many pleasures of this activity, but we are not willing to expose ourselves to excessive or unnecessary danger.

Unfortunately, some riders act in ways that make riding riskier. Those who use motorcycling to get an adrenaline rush have an attitude toward risk that often leads to rashed bodywork and broken bodies. Pushing your limits can be an exhilarating experience, but defying the bounds of reason or control is often short-lived folly.

Equally risky is drinking and riding. Depending on which statistics you read, alcohol use contributes to 30 to 50% of motorcycle fatalities. A couple of drinks may not seem like a big deal, but even a little bit of alcohol can affect your control and judgement, and give you an inflated sense of confidence that can easily lead to a fatal mistake. It's important to recognize the dangers of peer pressure, particularly when it leads to riding while under the influence of substances. I strongly recommend that you separate drinking and riding.

High-risk behavior puts not only you in danger, it also affects those around you. It's easy to think you're the only one affected by poor risk management and bad judgement, but your risky behavior can affect other riders or drivers who get caught up in your mistakes. Also, keep in mind that your risky behavior will impact your loved ones who must take care of you when you get hurt.

It's obvious that overtly risky behavior can lead to injury, but there are many less obvious situations that present a high level of risk. For instance, riding in the rain with bald tires or accelerating through intersections trying to beat a red traffic light are two behaviors that carry a high risk of injury.

↘ risk profile assessment

To help you recognize your current level of risk exposure, complete the "Risk Profile Assessment" by circling the number that describes your *typical* behavior.

When complete, add up the numbers you circled to determine your risk exposure profile. A score of 10 to 22 indicates "least risk." A score of 23 to 37 indicates "moderate risk." A score of 38 to 50 indicates "high risk."

If you're not comfortable with the results, maybe it's time to make some changes.

Points	5	4	3	2	1
Helmet Use	Never	Sometimes	Always Non-DOT	Always Open-faced Helmet	Always Full-faced
Wear Full-Coverage Riding Gear	Never	Rarely	Sometimes	Frequently	Always
Rider Training	None	MSF Beginner in distant past	Recent MSF Beginner or ERC	MSF and Frequent Practice	MSF, Practice, and Track School
Parking Lot Practice	Never	Rarely	Sometimes	Often	Frequently
Ride at Night	Often	Occasionally	Sometimes	Rarely	Never
Pass on Double Yellow	Often	Occasionally	Sometimes	Rarely	Never
Influenced by Peer Pressure	Often	Occasionally	Sometimes	Rarely	Never
Utilize Strategies for Being Seen	Never	Rarely	Sometimes	Frequently	Always
Riding and Alcohol	Occasionally	Rarely	After waiting 1 hour/drink	After waiting 2 hours/drink	Never
Exceed Speed Limit by More Than 15 mph	Often	Occasionally	Sometimes	Rarely	Never

mental factors in managing risk

Frequent close calls with traffic or running wide in corners are two clues that indicate weak mental preparation for managing risk. Many motorcycle accidents occur because the rider failed to observe the situation ahead or accurately predict what was about to happen. Multi-vehicle crashes can be avoided with keen environmental awareness to identify and predict threatening traffic movement. Single-vehicle crashes usually occur in corners and can be prevented by evaluating common cornering problems and establishing accurate entry speeds.

situational awareness

Managing risk requires tuning into your environment. This means having a high level of awareness, attention, and focus that allows you to identify and interpret subtle information that can hint at a potentially dangerous situation. How aware are you of your surroundings? To what degree can you take small clues and "connect the dots" to identify potential hazards? Are you conscious of your intuition? Answers to these questions can help you to identify your level of "situational awareness."

Situational awareness is the ability to accurately perceive information about your environment based on knowledge and understanding. A well-developed situational awareness means you are able to "see the big picture" so you can identify when something in your field of view seems "out of place." It also means accurately evaluating likely outcomes and responding quickly to minimize the threat.

Imagine entering an intersection with several cars waiting to turn. You notice a slight movement and reflection from a windshield to your left. You respond to the visual warning by slowing, covering your brakes, and moving to the right, away from the hazard. You avoid the inattentive driver with little drama, turning an otherwise close call into a barely-notable event.

multitasking

Closely related to situational awareness is the ability to multitask. Riding a motorcycle requires you to combine mental information-processing functions and physical motorcycle control actions. These tasks overlap continuously as we deal with traffic, carve through a series of corners, or simply cruise down the highway. An efficient, well-developed ability to multitask maintains a reserve of brain capacity for dealing with multiple events that have the potential to result in a crash.

Multitasking is necessary in order to ride a motorcycle safely, but multitasking can increase your risk if you try to do too much at once. Recent studies have concluded that a continuous state of managing simultaneous actions leads to an overstimulated mind that is unable to focus deeply. One task is sacrificed as another is introduced, which in turn is cut short as a third task is taken on.

The trick is to learn to perform multiple tasks, but not so many that you become over-whelmed. Recognize your current capacity for multitasking and keep the number of tasks you handle within your ability.

prioritizing

You can't expect to devote equal attention to several potential hazards, therefore it's important to identify and evaluate each risk and de-termine whether or not a hazard is significant. You must avoid the trap of devoting too much attention to a hazard with relatively little risk while missing a more critical danger. For in-stance, focusing undue attention on a small patch of sand while ignoring a large truck crossing your path would be unwise. The best riders give a potential hazard only the amount of attention it deserves; no more, no less.

Crashes are usually the product of several events that occur one at a time in rapid suc-cession. Keep your eyes constantly moving to identify and evaluate potential problems. Prioritize the hazards and act efficiently to stop the hazardous sequence from progressing.

Risk directly affects your riding pleasure; high-risk situations cause stress and detract from enjoyment. While you can't eliminate risk you can learn to minimize it by accurately recognizing your level of risk exposure, increasing your environmental awareness, and learning to give each hazard the correct amount of attention. Each of these strategies woven together create a formidable force to reduce risk and increase the likelihood of zone experiences.

mental skill development
taking command of the environment

part II

Now that you have a clearer understanding of factors needed to ride with confidence, we can turn to managing the riding environment. This includes developing strategies for minimizing hazards, improving visual skills, and establishing a strong understanding of traction. Thorough comprehension of these topics will lead to increased safety and a deeper, more satisfying connection to motorcycling through increased confidence and a greater sense of control.

4

Contrary to what most people think, motorcycling is more mental than it is physical. Sure, the ability to ride a motorcycle well requires coordination and refined motor skills, but without an intimate knowledge of your environment and without specific strategies to minimize hazards you are at a significant disadvantage. You also need fortitude to use good sense and to resist influences that can easily get you into trouble.

Riding becomes much safer and more fun if your mind has a firm grasp on how to master the environment in which you ride. This means being aware of the most risky situations and having a preconceived plan for how to survive them.

adopt the common strategies

Here are a few common strategies used by expert riders to manage risk.

Ride like you are invisible. It's foolish to assume that drivers will see you or behave as you expect. To help drivers see you, choose lane positions and following distances that afford maximum sight distance (see following page).

Wearing brightly colored clothing and a conspicuous helmet can help to make you visible. Burning your headlight provides good conspicuity, but consider the problems with using your high beams during the day: the bright light can obscure your profile and make it harder for traffic to judge your speed and distance and can make turn signals hard to see.

Finally, understand that being seen is the most reliable way to alert drivers of your presence. Don't rely on your horn or loud pipes to let other drivers know you are there.

Have an out. Smart riders choose lane positions that avoid traffic conflicts and provide a way out in case something bad happens. For instance, to prevent being "pinched" between merging highway traffic on your right and vehicles traveling on your left, move out of the right-hand lane when approaching on-ramps. To avoid being rear-ended when stopped at a traffic light, it is wise to position yourself off-center of the car ahead so you can maneuver around it if a vehicle fails to stop from behind. When riding through intersections, look for escape routes that you can use, just in case.

Ride within your limits. While this good advice is hard to dispute, it can be difficult to know where your limits lie. To ride safely you must develop an accurate assessment of your abilities. Many riders discover the limit of their abilities when they encounter the "panic test." If you feel anxiety, you're close to the edge. If you feel panic, you're already there. Panic must be avoided, because the natural human response to panic is to overreact, which often leads to a crash. A mismatch between your abilities and the challenges you encounter undermines your sense of security and kills confidence.

Ask yourself 'What if?' Imagine you are approaching an intersection with a truck in the opposite lane waiting to turn left across your path. What would you do if the truck were to suddenly turn. Where would you go? Would it be better to stop, swerve, or accelerate? Imagine the scenario in detail and solve the problem several different ways. Then ask yourself whether you have the skills to execute all of the maneuvers required to avoid a crash. If not, then you would be wise to overcome your weaknesses so that when these skills are needed you will be ready.

choose favorable lane positioning

Lane positioning is an important means for making yourself seen and for seeing hazards. When riding behind a vehicle it's often best to position yourself in the left-hand portion of your lane so oncoming drivers can see you. When vehicles you are following block the view of drivers who are waiting to enter the roadway from the right you may need to move to the right portion of your lane to give the waiting driver a clear view of you. Cars and trucks also block our view of potential hazards. Proper lane positioning allows you to look past these vehicles to see hazards more easily.

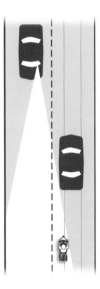

You should position yourself to maintain space between you and hazards. For instance, move away from cars wanting to turn across your lane and steer clear of possible surface hazards. This process of changing lane positions occurs continuously. Learn to recognize the best lane position to provide optimum conspicuity and visibility and to cushion yourself from dangers.

Set your lane position to maintain a safe distance behind the vehicle ahead. A good rule of thumb is to stay at least two seconds behind. Doing so will give you a better line of sight to the road ahead, it will give other drivers a better view of you, and it will give you time and space to react if the driver ahead stops or turns quickly.

riding gear

Another kind of risk reduction strategy is to minimize injury in the event of a crash by wearing sturdy protective riding gear. Of course, wearing protective gear will not in itself make you a better rider or prevent a crash from happening. But, considering that a simple tipover at 20 mph can result in a lot of pain and a likely emergency room visit for an unprotected rider, it is in your best interest to wear a helmet, jacket, gloves, pants, and boots that offer both comfort and protection.

You won't wear riding gear if it doesn't meet your fashion or comfort standards, so shop around before buying. Hot weather is one of the favorite excuses for not wearing protective gear. Happily, there are many jackets and pants on the market that provide very good venting to make riding in steamy weather quite comfortable.

Some riders wear minimal protective gear because they want to project a certain image. If you dislike wearing a full-face helmet, then wear a DOT-approved open-face helmet made by a reputable manufacturer. Avoid the novelty "beanie" helmets that offer little-to-no protection.

Black leather is the material of choice for many riders, but be aware that black won't stand out in traffic. A light-colored helmet can offset this by offering some conspicuity. But, the best combination for being visible is a bright-colored jacket *and* helmet. Choose to protect yourself and increase conspicuity to minimize the risk of injury and increase your sense of well-being.

Each of the riders below has a different idea of proper riding gear.

high risk situations

What follows are situations I've singled out because of the increased risk they pose. Recognizing these problem scenarios before you encounter them can help you to be better prepared.

invaders

One of the most common traffic hazards you face as a motorcyclist is an oncoming driver who turns left across your lane at an intersection. It's not as though these drivers are out to deliberately kill you. Most are responsible and attentive, but sometimes they make poor decisions, often because they simply don't see you, or they do see you but make an inaccurate judgement about your approach speed and distance from the intersection.

As I said earlier, you can help drivers see you better by making yourself as conspicuous as possible. You need to do more than simply ride with your headlight on and wear bright clothing. You must also use effective lane positioning so drivers can easily recognize your presence; you can't expect a driver in oncoming traffic to see you if you are riding close behind a large truck.

To ensure that drivers don't invade your right of way it's important to ride at "expected" speeds. This means approaching intersections at a speed that surrounding drivers can easily judge. If you ride toward intersections at elevated speeds you can surely expect to have many close calls and an eventual crash.

surface hazards

Without traction you can't steer, brake, or even stay upright, which is why road surface hazards are such a concern. Loose debris such as sand or gravel can appear anywhere, but are most likely to appear near construction zones, at road edges, and in intersections. In the northern states where sand is used to enhance winter traction you can expect to find sand-covered roads on early springtime rides.

There are many other surface hazards, such as crack sealer ("tar snakes"), construction plates, railroad tracks, manhole covers, diesel spills—the list goes on and on. It takes constant diligence to spot these hazards so you can minimize the risk they pose.

The best way to manage surface hazards is to avoid them. Of course, that isn't always possible. When you must ride over loose surfaces do so smoothly. Slow before you reach the hazard and avoid braking or turning until you are past the debris. If you come across a surface hazard in the middle of a corner that you cannot avoid, it's best to straighten the motorcycle, ride over the slippery stuff, then get back into the lean when you are once again on clean pavement. That way, you'll minimize the risk of a slide.

groups

In Chapter 2, I described how peer pressure can threaten your well-being and how "pack" influence can cause the most risk-averse riders to act out of character and outside their comfort zone. If you've ever ridden with a group of riders who speed, pass aggressively, or block traffic then you know what I mean.

The easy answer is to avoid riding in groups, but that solution limits this enjoyable social aspect of motorcycling. Another solution is to choose new riding companions who have sensible attitudes toward risk and who are able to resist the temptation of high-risk, pack-driven conduct. If neither of these solutions will work for you, then consider riding in the back of the pack where you can separate yourself from aggressive behavior.

There are other dangers with group riding, such as aggressive, erratic, or inexperienced riders causing multi-bike crashes. Evaluate which riders might be a problem and stay away from them. Finally, recognize the risks of an unexpected on-road encounter with another motorcyclist where the temptation can be high to "show your stuff."

speeding

Whether you are riding in a group or individually, speeding will likely lead to unfortunate outcomes. Under ideal conditions, stopping at 30 mph takes roughly 35 feet; stopping at 60 mph can take more than 140 feet. Yes, you read that correctly, the stopping distance is *four* times longer when your speed is doubled. Also consider that one second of reaction time equals 44 feet at 30 mph and 88 feet at 60 mph and you can see why riding at reasonable speeds is the first step in reducing risk.

Another reason for keeping speeds reasonable is so that surrounding traffic can judge your approach speed accurately. If you ride significantly faster than what is expected by other drivers, don't be surprised if they pull out in front of you thinking it is safe to proceed. This is particularly important in places where cars expect relatively slow traffic speeds, such as school zones and congested shopping areas. Note that because motorcycles are narrower than cars and often have only one headlight, it is more difficult to judge their speed when they are coming toward you.

Stretching your limits and the limits of your motorcycle can be stimulating, but riding fast on the street can easily turn from exhilarating to terrifying. Rounding a predictable corner at a certain speed may not challenge your cornering ability, but if the corner radius tightens un-expectedly or if an oil spill appears mid-corner, your skills may not be adequate. The answer is to ride in a way that reduces risk without eliminating the fun and exhilaration.

The good news is that the thrill and satisfaction of riding can be equally great when riding at slower speeds. Carving through a series of corners with absolute precision at a moderate pace is just as invigorating as ripping through the twisties near the ragged edge. It is very satisfying to place your front tire precisely at the corner entry and establish the exact lean an-gle necessary with as little mid-corner correction as possible while looking through the turn and smoothly accelerating to the exit. That's how you enjoy the rewards of riding without the risk of high speeds.

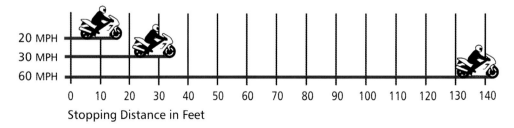

*When speed is doubled, stopping distance **quadruples**!*

passing and lane splitting

Riding behind a slow-moving vehicle on an otherwise superb stretch of road or being stuck in a traffic jam can be infuriating. Before you succumb to impatience and twist the throttle to get ahead, it is important to weigh the risks of passing and lane splitting.

The risk of passing on a wide-open road with plenty of sight distance and no intersecting side streets is relatively low. In contrast, passing in areas that have inadequate sight distance or multiple intersections can be quite risky. Drivers can suddenly emerge from intersecting roads and driveways, or the driver you are passing may suddenly decide to turn into one of them.

Carving skillfully through a vacant stretch of twisty tarmac unencumbered by traffic is fertile ground for an invigorating experience. Knowing this, it may be tempting to pass slower vehicles where it's not safe or legal in an attempt to maintain your rhythm. Choosing to pass when you are not 100 percent sure you can do so safely will increase anxiety.

When you do pass, choose speeds that balance risk exposure and legality. It's smart to keep passing speeds moderate, but it's not wise to pass at a speed just barely faster than the vehicle you're overtaking either. Doing so would leave you exposed in the oncoming lane for a longer period of time than if you use your bike's power to accelerate quickly around.

It is also important to weigh the risks associated with lane splitting. One argument in favor of lane splitting is that it is safer to ride between lanes than to be sandwiched between cars in stop-and-go traffic. This may have some truth, but lane splitting itself is risky. If you choose to split lanes, it is important to do so when traffic is rolling very slowly and to keep your speed down to within 5 mph or so of the slower traffic.

commuting

Commuting can be a risky venue where drivers impatiently jockey for position in traffic. Even though this setting doesn't seem conducive to enjoyable riding, managing these challenges successfully can be quite satisfying.

Commuting offers the perfect opportunity to play the imaginary video game mentioned in Chapter 1 where errant drivers are challenges you must predict and overcome. To play the game well requires being immersed in the moment to allow full awareness of your surroundings. You accumulate "points" with each hazard you successfully predict and avoid. Extra points are won by helping traffic see you so they never become hazards. A well-played game increases enjoyment and builds confidence in your ability to master your riding environment.

The trick to dealing with commuter traffic is to maximize your conspicuity to other drivers and maintain a margin of space around you. As narrow, single-track vehicles, motorcycles have the advantage of using the left, center, and right portions of the lane. This allows you

↘ on your next ride, let them go

If a slow driver is ruining your run through a favorite section of road, consider pulling over and waiting a minute or so instead of making an aggressive or potentially risky pass. This will provide some distance between you and the slow vehicle. Once the car is far enough ahead, proceed to ride at your preferred pace until you catch up to the vehicle once again. This technique allows you to enjoy your own rhythm without the stress of risky passing.

to maintain a safety zone away from vehicles around you. It's also important to maintain a minimum two-second following distance and keep your motorcycle moving through blind spots. Stay alert for any unusual movements in front, behind, and to the sides. (See the next chapter for more on visual skills.)

In some places the density and aggressive nature of commuter traffic ruins any chance of an enjoyable ride. In this case, you are better off taking an alternative route that avoids the worst traffic, even if it takes a bit longer to get to your destination. This way, you'll reduce your exposure to commuter hazards and increase your chances of an enjoyable ride.

rain riding

Difficult situations such as rain riding demand your full attention. All other thoughts must be put aside and your tactile senses and concentration must be acutely focused. Rain riding may not be your idea of fun, but successfully handling challenging situations such as this lead to greater confidence—as long as you are mentally and physically prepared.

Being prepared for adverse conditions is the hallmark of a happy rider. There is nothing more satisfying than being warm and dry in your rainsuit while slicing skillfully through steady rain knowing that your preparation has kept you comfortable and reduced the likelihood of dangerous distraction.

To improve the likelihood of a satisfying experience, you need to have confidence that your tires will grip. When riding in the rain, your braking, turning, and accelerating need to be done smoothly to ensure adequate traction. Gentle inputs allow your weight to shift gradually so traction is maintained.

Rain-soaked pavement retains about 70 to 80 percent of the friction of clean, dry pavement, which means that traction is plentiful for most situations; however, many roadways are anything but clean. Vehicles drip, spit, and dribble all sorts of goop that accumulates between rainstorms to form a slimy mess when mixed with water.

That stuff can easily cause a slide. The best way to remove this residue is for a downpour to wash it away. This cleaning process can take a while depending on how long it's been since the last rainstorm and the amount of crud that has formed. Be especially smooth when braking, turning, or accelerating during this time to avoid losing traction—or better yet, sit out the beginning of a storm.

Reduce speed to maintain traction and reduce the chance of hydroplaning. Hydroplaning occurs when a layer of water forms between your tires and the road, causing the tire to skate over the road surface. This can happen if you ride through standing water at too high a speed or if your tire tread is too worn to expel the water. Keep your tires properly inflated and replace them well before they are worn enough that the tread wear indicators contact the road.

Being seen and seeing hazards is another common problem when riding in rain. Not only does the rain obscure vision as it beats down on windshields and face shields, it also obscures road hazards. Make sure you are prepared with eye protection that provides the best visibility possible, such as a clear or amber-tinted face shield. Also, cool, moist air can cause fogging. Using an anti-fogging product, such as Fog City®, can help. Being seen by other drivers is difficult enough even in dry weather, so it's not surprising that others will have a tough time seeing you when visibility is reduced by rain. Reflective material on your helmet and riding gear can go a long way toward making you conspicuous to other drivers.

Even if you consciously choose to avoid rain riding you can unexpectedly find yourself wet and miserable; precipitation can fall at any time. You can make a rain ride tolerable—or even enjoyable—by accepting the situation. You can't do anything about the weather, so you may as well make the best of it. With extra care and awareness, rain riding can be a satisfying experience. With the assurance that you are prepared if it does rain, you can enjoy perfectly good riding days with less-than-ideal forecasts.

night riding

Riding takes on a different quality at night as your headlight guides you through the darkness. But night riding can raise your anxiety for the unexpected. Riding within the limits of this tricky environment and utilizing a few strategies can make riding at night a lot of fun.

Of course, it's the inability to see far ahead that offers the biggest challenge to night-time riding. The Motorcycle Safety Foundation suggests scanning 12 seconds ahead. But headlights can't light that far ahead when you are moving at 40 or 50 mph. This means that many hazards appear suddenly. Make sure your attention is razor sharp and scan aggressively for surface hazards as well as animals that tend to move around at night.

One obvious strategy for night riding is to slow down. To help increase your nighttime sight distance, use the headlights of cars ahead of you. Also, use the tail and brake lights of these vehicles as an early warning for curves, dips, and obstacles. It's also important to maximize your ability to see by keeping eye protection clean and scratch-free. Even light scratches can impair nighttime vision as oncoming headlights turn into distracting flares.

Seeing where you're going is important, but it's equally important to be seen, so you should make an extra effort to help drivers see you at night. Wear light-colored riding gear with reflective material on your jacket and helmet. If black leather is your garment of choice then consider wearing a reflective vest for those night rides.

Strategies to minimize risk are developed over time. Begin by making the strategies described in this chapter an integral part of your subconscious so you automatically use them on every ride.

5

Being seen and being able to see hazards is critical for safety. Your most important and reliable sense for assessing danger accurately is your eyesight. Our eyes scan the riding environment and make a "visual map," which allows our brain to tell us whether the "picture" hints of a threat or not. Visual information tells you whether you are riding too fast for an approaching corner or if a car is about to collide with you.

With proper training we can become more observant of our surroundings, to pick up subtle visual cues that would otherwise go unnoticed. Enhanced sensory conditioning leads to a greater feeling of control, higher confidence, and a more intimate connection with the environment. This chapter discusses the nature of vision as it pertains to riding and offers specific suggestions that can help you increase your visual acuity.

look for trouble

It's not enough simply to look ahead. You must practice visual attentiveness and actively search for hazards by keeping your eyes moving, never fixating on a single object for more than a couple of seconds. By scanning continually your mind can assess multiple hazards in a short amount of time.

It's important to scan well ahead. Riders who limit their scanning to the near distance undermine their confidence, because they are surprised by obstacles or road characteristics that appear "suddenly." Conversely, riders who have trained themselves to keep their eyes up and their vision high and wide are able to see hazards much earlier to allow ample time and space to respond. This skill alone will lead to a more relaxed ride and improve your confidence.

To understand how the brain processes visual information, it's helpful to understand the difference between *looking, noticing,* and *perceiving.* You *look* in the direction where dangers appear, *notice* that potential hazards are present, and *perceive* whether the hazard poses enough danger to warrant evasive action. Looking is mostly a mechanical activity and noticing is what happens when an object gets your attention, but visual perception is the brain's response that tells you what needs to be done and helps you to execute needed maneuvers skillfully.

Proficient visual acuity is more than simply looking. It also involves noticing threats and perceiving their risk potential.

traffic vision

Riding in traffic requires a heightened visual sense. Aggressively scan for anomalies in typical traffic flow patterns. The majority of hazards come from ahead, but it's important to check to the sides and behind for errant drivers. Also, be sure to monitor your mirrors when stopped in traffic and remain in first gear until the traffic behind is stopped, in case a quick getaway is necessary.

Not everyone on the road has the same level of visual awareness. People are as attentive as they feel they need to be, which is why car drivers, in their protective metal compartments, often miss important visual cues that can prevent accidents. Motorcycles are relatively small and are perceived as a minor threat to drivers. This makes motorcycles less likely to be noticed and is a major reason why car drivers commonly invade motorcyclists' right-of-way.

Take a look at the pattern of circles in the diagrams on this page. There are two identically-sized circles centrally located in both diagrams. In the top diagram smaller circles surround the center circle, and in the bottom diagram larger circles surround the center circle. Notice how the circle in the center of the top diagram appears larger than the central circle in the bottom diagram even though they are indeed the same size. This shows how a motorcycle may appear smaller than it actually is—and psychologically less significant—when surrounded by large vehicles.

Unfortunately, with the aging of the general population and the increased use of mobile electronics, we can expect more drivers to be less attentive and responsive to difficult traffic situations. Your best bet is to ride at appropriate and expected speeds, wear bright-colored clothing, and position yourself in traffic for maximum conspicuity—and expect that you might not be seen.

speed vision

At faster speeds your visual processing must be very efficient. This means looking farther ahead, scanning more aggressively, and processing information very quickly. You will certainly feel overwhelmed if your riding speed exceeds your ability to process information rapidly enough. If you feel anxious in traffic the best solution is to slow down and refocus your vision well ahead to permit early identification of road characteristics and traffic hazards.

Scanning the distant horizon allows early data gathering and minimizes speed-induced anxiety. When you look down at the road, speed is accentuated as the road rushes beneath your tires. In contrast, the landscape appears to pass at a slower rate when your vision is focused in the distance.

corner vision

Skillful cornering requires accurate visual information about a corner's radius, camber, and surface quality. With this information you can evaluate a corner's unique characteristics and come up with a "cornering plan," which is discussed in Chapter 8.

To help determine a corner's radius you can use the visual information provided by the white painted fog lines or the road edge. Notice how the white lines converge in the distance at a "vanishing point." If the lines converge quickly and in the near distance, then you can count on a tightening corner radius, whereas a distant vanishing point indicates a straighter radius. This information can also help you determine road slope and camber.

Identifying a corner's radius is important to determine whether your pace is suitable for safe cornering. A too-fast entry speed is the reason for most single-vehicle crashes as the panicked rider freezes and runs off the road or grabs the brakes and crashes.

Once in the curve, keep your eyes looking well ahead to identify what's coming up and to spot mid-corner hazards. It's also important to monitor possible surface hazards using quick downward glances. Continually gather information from near and far with an upward and downward search pattern.

visual direction control

Another reason to look well ahead through corners is to help direct your motorcycle where you want it to go. This is commonly known as "visual direction control," essentially your eyes telling your mind where you want the motorcycle to go next.

You feel much more in control when you actively point your eyes and attention through corners. The result is a motorcycle that feels easier to turn. Of course, it takes more than simply looking in a certain direction to make a motorcycle turn, but visual direction control contributes significantly to cornering confidence.

⬂ on your next ride

To make visual direction control a bigger part of your visual skill set, consciously scan farther ahead through turns. Look into the curve before leaning, then turn your head and move your vision along the desired cornering path all the way to the corner exit. Look down briefly to monitor the surface condition, but keep the majority of your vision high where you can see hazards and direct your motorcycle. Notice how your motorcycle seems to turn more easily and how cornering appears less threatening. Look where you want to go!

seek desirable visual targets

Visual direction control is a powerful aid for directing your motorcycle, but it can be hazardous if your eyes fix on a *hazard*—a common reaction to panic. "Target fixation" is the term used to describe this panic response. Fixing your eyes and attention on a hazard tends to steer your motorcycle directly toward where you *fear* to go rather than where you *want* to go.

Entering corners at excessive speed is a common source of panic that leads to target fixation, as the panicked rider fixes his or her attention on the opposite lane or the side of the road. The result often leads to the motorcycle heading directly toward the oncoming lane or road shoulder. To prevent this often-tragic result it is important to consciously choose desirable visual targets—in this case, the corner exit. Focus on the solution, not the problem. This takes practice and determination to perform consistently.

Target fixation also occurs in traffic. A common scenario is that an oncoming vehicle performs an unexpected, threatening maneuver, such as turning left across your lane. A rider who cannot resist visually targeting the hazard will often drive into the vehicle, even though they may have been able to steer around it if they had spotted an escape route.

Even traffic traveling in the same direction can present the possibility of target fixation. Look past cars you are following to avoid fixing on their rear taillight; this allows you to see hazards well ahead and plan accordingly. Motorcyclists riding in groups can present target fixation hazards as well. Take a cue from racers who focus their attention past their competitors to the track ahead in order to maintain their desired path and prevent crashing into a falling rider.

↘ on your next ride

Minimize the likelihood of target fixation by consciously looking toward the escape route around obstacles you encounter on your next ride, such as a stick or a manhole cover. Identify the problem, then quickly look for the solution.

vision blockers

There are many factors that affect your ability to see clearly and limit your information gathering capability. Fatigue or inattention can severely affect your ability to process visual information accurately; so can environmental conditions, such as solar glare, rain, or fog. Self-inflicted impairments, such as alcohol consumption or wearing tinted eye protection at night can also severely affect your visual acuity.

Eyesight generally deteriorates as we age and can affect visual processing time. You may not notice diminished eyesight, but be aware of subtle changes and have your eyes examined periodically to ensure optimum performance.

↘ on your next ride

Improved visual acuity begins by being aware of your current habits. On your next ride, notice how efficiently you gather visual information. Strive to purposefully expand your visual field to take in information from a "broader window." Train yourself to recognize objects that take an excessive amount of attention and consciously look away, toward a desirable path.

visual practice

Here are two simple exercises to help you expand your focal awareness. The first exercise will help you recognize subtle peripheral information. The second exercise will help you to target objects while noticing your surroundings.

Look up from this page at a distant object. Observe surrounding objects within your whole field of view without looking directly at them. Recognize the diminishing amounts of detail from your central focus to your periphery. Repeat this exercise periodically to train your brain to include information outside your central vision and to effectively widen your visual range.

Next, look into the distance and target several different objects. Rapidly scan between these objects in a random side to side and up and down pattern. Stop only momentarily to notice basic detail, such as texture or shape. While focusing on each target object, notice additional objects within your wide field of view. The idea is to observe individual objects while being aware of the whole environment; this is helpful when you are faced with multiple hazards.

By understanding the limits of your vision and practicing visual awareness, you can improve your visual acuity. Train yourself to master a wide field of vision to increase awareness of your surroundings without diverting your eyes from the desired path. Most importantly, keep your eyes moving. It takes continual, aggressive searching and scanning to gather information effectively.

With keen visual skills you will be able to anticipate problems and respond calmly. An unexpected bend in the road is noticed early and handled smoothly because you recognized subtle clues about the road ahead; a distant shadow shows signs of danger, alerting you to the shaded damp pavement and the need for a slight change of direction. Highly developed visual skills also keep your focus and attention "in the moment," allowing your mind to be quiet and your senses sharply attuned to your surroundings. The feeling of confidence you gain improves your ability to respond to sudden changes and reinforces your sense of mastery and well-being.

6

Riding in the zone requires a well developed "traction sense." A keen awareness of the quality and quantity of available traction allows you to predict whether grip is adequate and allows you to respond appropriately. This sense gives you assurance that you can manage available traction in most, if not all, situations and leads to a deep feeling of confidence.

Many riders take traction for granted, until it becomes scarce. Having an acute sense of available traction gives you a feeling of communication with the road and lets you ride more securely.

developing a traction sense

To develop a traction sense, it is important to understand what traction is and what affects traction quality and quantity. With this information, you'll recognize situations where traction is likely to be abundant and where it is not, so you can act in a way that maintains control. Over time, you'll develop a traction sense that is as transparent and effective as your sense of smell, touch, or sight.

traction feedback

A well-developed traction sense requires a high level of attentiveness, allowing you to tune in to the interaction between your tires and the road. Riding in the zone requires that you recognize and translate these subtle cues. For instance, slight changes in handlebar feel may indicate that front tire grip is at its limit. A slight wiggle or feeling of vagueness in your seat and foot pegs can indicate that the rear tire is losing grip.

It may be helpful to think of traction feedback as a "slip sense." When traction is sufficient for safety and control, your senses tell you that all is well; the motion of your motorcycle matches your intentions and expectations; you sense no tire slipping or sliding as you brake or corner. But, when traction is beginning to diminish, your nerves sense a sudden change in the connection between the tires and the road with the motorcycle moving uneasily beneath you.

You sense much of this feedback through the handlebars. A tight grip and stiff arms hamper your ability to feel what the bike is doing. To detect the subtlest bits of feedback, relax your arms and hands as much as possible. You can also take a cue from racers and select gloves with thin, yet durable material to maximize the sensitivity between handle grip and the nerves in your hand.

Feedback about traction comes from the nerves in your feet, butt, and hands. Thin, yet sturdy gloves can help access feedback.

recognizing traction quality

Traction is a gripping force between the tire contact patch and the road surface. Several things affect how much traction is available, including road and tire temperature, road condition, surface texture, tire compound, tire wear, and the amount of "load" pressing the tires onto the road surface.

It's important to develop a sharp eye for evaluating surface quality, because traction is closely related to variations in road surface characteristics. One significant characteristic that affects grip is *surface texture.* A coarse texture offers the best traction for the rubber to mechanically interlock with the abundant dimples and voids of the surface, whereas smooth surfaces such as manhole covers and painted markings offer less grip. Other road features that provide poor traction include crack filler, loose gravel or dirt, and steel construction plates. Milled or scarified pavement found at construction zones may be very rough, but offer less-than-ideal grip due to the large depressions where the tires have no significant contact.

Changes in road color offer clues about whether the surface is smooth or coarse. A coarse surface often looks dull, whereas a smooth surface typically has a high contrast, glossy look.

Timing of rider inputs is critical for managing traction. Sometimes, you must delay braking, turning, or accelerating until you reach a place when traction is adequate. For instance, attempting to brake or turn over a wet manhole cover would be unwise.

Moisture and surface debris reduce the amount of available traction no matter what surface you're on. Slow down and scan far ahead to avoid last-minute maneuvers such as swerving or emergency stops. If you encounter debris while in a turn, straighten before you reach the debris, then return to the lean as soon as traction permits. Make sure your tires are in good condition and your inputs are smooth and gradual to maintain traction when the road turns wet or dirty.

⬎ traction circle

The traction circle diagram is helpful for explaining the concept of variable traction quantity. The radius of the circle represents total available traction. The red vertical arrow indicates braking force and the blue horizontal arrow indicates side force required for cornering. The green arrow represents the result of the combined braking and cornering force, or total tire force.

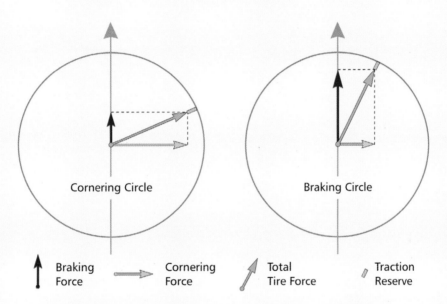

Notice in the "cornering circle" that the vertical arrow (braking forces) must be shorter to allow the horizontal arrow (cornering forces) to become longer and have the green Total Tire Force line remain inside the circle.

In the "braking circle" there is little cornering force available when the brakes are applied hard as indicated by the short horizontal arrow (cornering forces) and the long vertical arrow (braking forces). This is why attempting to corner or swerve while braking hard is a bad idea.

It wouldn't be smart to ride at the very edge of traction, so in typical riding situations all of the arrow ends should stay well inside the circle's edge, indicating traction *reserve*. Traction reserve is important for managing surprise hazards. If the green Total Tire Force line extends outside the circle then traction is lost.

traction users

There are three basic actions that use traction: acceleration, turning, and braking. *Driving forces* from acceleration can spin the rear wheel, *side forces* from cornering can cause a slide, and *braking force* can cause a skid as forward inertia is halted.

Any one of these forces can eat up the entire allotment of available grip; executing any two of these actions at the same time can easily lead to a fall unless they are managed carefully. In other words, if you use 90 percent of the available traction for braking, there is only 10 percent traction remaining to turn or perform an evasive maneuver such as a swerve. It takes a keen traction sense to balance available traction.

traction and load

Understanding how load affects traction can help you sharpen your traction sense. Traction quality (potential) is dependent on tire compound and surface condition, while traction quantity is largely determined by how much weight is pressing the tires onto and into the road surface.

To feel this effect, slide your hand across a table surface using little downward force; you'll feel little resistance and your hand slides easily. Now, attempt to slide your hand across the table while pressing downward; feel the increased surface friction. This is essentially what happens with your tires under load.

At rest, a motorcycle's weight is supported about evenly by each tire. Braking and accelerating shift the load forward or backward—forward under braking and backward when accelerating. This means that front tire load and traction *increase* when the brakes are applied, but *decrease* under acceleration. Conversely, rear tire load and traction *increase* when accelerating, but *decrease* under braking. Even though additional load increases traction, too much braking or driving force can overwhelm a tire's ability to grip the road. The result is a front tire skid or a rear wheel spin.

Traction and control are directly affected by how skillfully you manage these shifts in load. Allow time for load and traction to increase by accelerating gradually and squeezing the front brake lever progressively. Braking is discussed in more detail in Chapter 7.

Load Transfer While Braking

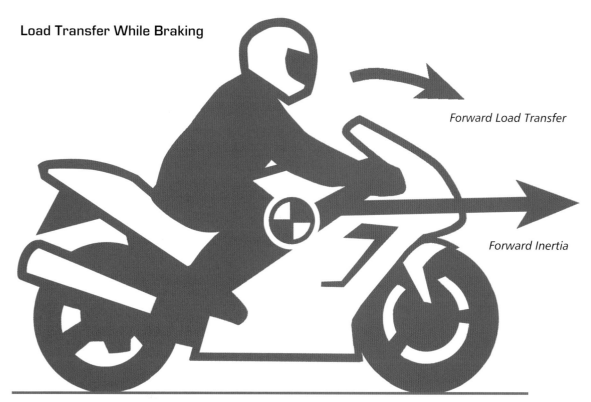

Forward Load Transfer

Forward Inertia

Rear Tire – Decreased Load and Traction　　　*Front Tire – Increased Load and Traction*

front rebound damping

front preload

suspension setup for traction

A well-adjusted suspension system keeps the tires in contact with the road for maximum traction. In order to keep the tires in contact with the pavement, the suspension must have the ability to rise over bumps and drop into surface depressions. To manage the various types of irregularities in the road surface, the forks and shock must respond by compressing and rebounding through a portion of their travel and at the proper rate.

Unfortunately, suspension adjustments are a mystery to most people. It's not unusual for riders never to move the preload or damping adjusters from the factory settings. In some cases this is fine, but those who take the time to understand how their motorcycle's suspension works are often able to improve handling with a few simple suspension adjustments. These riders discover that finely adjusted suspension leads to improved feedback and a greater sense of control.

Spring preload is adjusted to keep the springs in the middle of their travel. Factory preload settings may need to be adjusted for heavier riders and for accommodating the extra weight of passengers. Refer to your owner's manual for recommended settings and for the preload adjustment procedure (spring compression or air). For a more custom setting, measure the amount the springs compress (sag). This involves measuring the fork and swingarm travel from fully extended to where the spring is compressed with the rider on board. A typical street motorcycle sag measurement is around 30mm to 45mm. The precise process for adjusting sag is beyond the scope of this book, so I recommend you do some research to learn the proper method before undertaking this level of adjustment. If your springs are near either extreme end of their adjustment after measuring and adjusting your spring preload then you should look into replacing the stock springs with softer or firmer springs from the aftermarket.

front compression damping

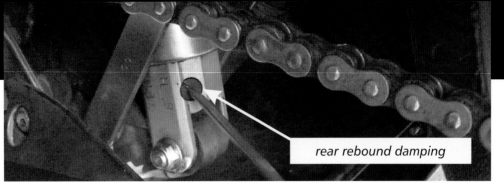

rear rebound damping

Some motorcycles have damping adjustments that affect spring rebound and compression rates. Compression damping controls front-end dive and the absorption of bumps, while rebound damping affects the spring's return rate. Less compression damping allows the spring to compress more easily and less rebound damping allows the spring to return more quickly after being compressed. Too little compression damping can result in excessive fork dive and too little rebound damping can cause the springs to extend excessively and the motorcycle to feel unstable.

Riders who develop a sharp sensitivity for the subtleties of suspension action can feel whether compression damping is too soft or too hard and whether the springs are rebounding too quickly or too slowly. With this information they are able to tune the forks and shock to achieve confidence-inspiring stability and maximum contact between their tires and the road.

Do yourself a favor and learn about your bike's suspension. Your owner's manual is a good place to start. It will describe the location of basic suspension adjusters, their purpose, and what the factory settings are. Once you have an understanding of each adjuster's function you are ready to experiment. Write down the current settings in case you want to return to them, then turn the adjusters and go for a ride. You may want to carry a screwdriver in your bag so you can stop occasionally to make changes. You may be surprised at the improvement you can achieve with well-adjusted suspension and you may be rewarded with greater confidence and a feeling of "oneness" with your bike.

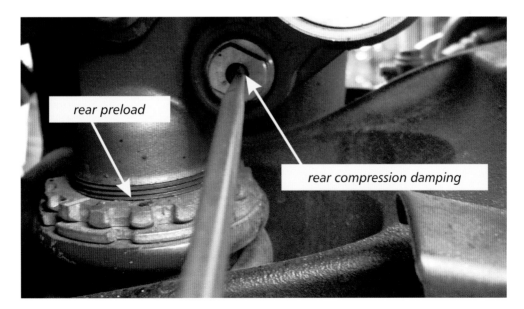

rear preload

rear compression damping

tires

Your tires connect your motorcycle to the road, and with a contact patch the size of the palm of your hand you are smart to not ignore the importance of tire selection and condition. Tire construction and compound, operating temperature, and overall condition all affect traction potential.

For best tire performance, maintain proper pressures. Correct tire pressure achieves the ideal balance between surface contact and temperature range. Failing to maintain proper pressures can lead to poor handling, accelerated wear, and even carcass delamination. Refer to your owner's manual for pressure specifications for various riding conditions, such as carrying heavy loads or a passenger. Tire pressures suitable for track days or racing will vary significantly from street pressures, so be sure to talk with your trackside vendor for advice.

Different tires have differing characteristics. Some tires (because of different profile shape) will let the motorcycle turn quicker at the expense of straight-line stability; some will absorb bumps better but give less feedback when cornering and braking. Take the opportunity to learn about and experiment with different tire brands and models to find a set that suits your personal preferences. Tires that don't feel right will detract you from maximum confidence and enjoyment.

It's also important to choose the tire that balances your needs for durability and for grip. Tires range from high-mileage types to ultra-soft race tires and everything in between.

Round Profile

Triangulated Profile

↘ types of tires

A Touring tires are designed to handle the weight of a heavy touring or cruiser motorcycle, luggage, and a passenger. These tires are made with harder rubber compounds that provide less grip compared to other tire types, but are more durable and last longer. Touring tires have a round profile for predictable cornering and straight-line stability at the expense of quick turning. They feature an abundance of rain-shedding grooves that minimize hydroplaning. Touring and cruiser tires can be either bias-ply or radial construction. Bias-ply tires operate differently from radial tires and therefore should not be interchanged with radials.

B Dual purpose tires are found on "adventure" and dual sport bikes. These tires have an aggressive tread pattern for grip on mild off-road terrain as well as pavement. Some dual sport tires are oriented more toward dirt and others more toward road use. Surprisingly, the road-oriented tires provide very good pavement traction as well as adequate off-road capability.

C Standard or sport touring tires are "do-it-all" tires. They have a round profile and offer very good grip along with comfortable stability and ample grooves for diverting water. They won't last as long as touring tires, but are a good choice for most street riders.

D Sport tires are designed for more aggressive street riders. These tires have fewer grooves for maximum dry-weather grip. Their soft rubber compound can easily squeeze deep into the surface texture, which provides superior grip at the expense of shorter life. Sport tires feature a sharper, triangulated profile with a smaller center contact area for quick turn-in and a broad side area for maximum contact at full lean. Several manufacturers offer "track day" tires that feature racetrack performance along with acceptable street characteristics.

E Race tires have few grooves, soft rubber, and a sharp profile to deliver high levels of grip and lightning fast turn-in. Carcass construction is designed for precise corner handling and feedback. Optimum traction lasts only a short time before performance begins to drop off.

   Using race compound tires as street tires is a waste of money and may even be hazardous. Race compound tires provide their superior grip within a narrow, high temperature range not achievable with typical street speeds. They also take a longer time to heat up compared with street tires and have few water-dispersing grooves. To attain maximum grip with acceptable street manners, consider "track day" tires.

F "Slicks" are the ultimate race tire; to achieve maximum contact, they have no water-dispersing grooves.

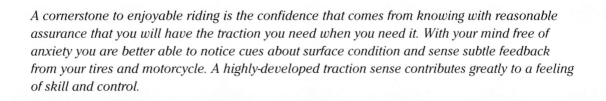

A cornerstone to enjoyable riding is the confidence that comes from knowing with reasonable assurance that you will have the traction you need when you need it. With your mind free of anxiety you are better able to notice cues about surface condition and sense subtle feedback from your tires and motorcycle. A highly-developed traction sense contributes greatly to a feeling of skill and control.

physical skill development
mastering motorcycle control

part III

A solid foundation of mental skills can lead to many happy miles as a motorcyclist. But, to enjoy riding you must also have confidence in your ability to control your motorcycle. This means developing solid physical skills, such as braking, cornering, and shifting. This section presents the foundations of motorcycle control and introduces some advanced techniques that can help you to move to a higher level of proficiency.

I have chosen the topics for this section carefully to be accessible to riders with an early-intermediate to early-advanced level of proficiency. Follow the text, then use the practice drills at the end of each chapter and on the DVD to help you turn these concepts into solid skills. Incorporating these techniques into your daily riding will help you become a better rider and increase your zone experiences.

7

It is obvious that proficient braking skills are critical for safety and control. In this chapter, you'll learn how to develop brake feel. You'll also learn the importance of the front brake, how to control the rear brake, and the fine points of emergency braking. I've also included several complex braking concepts that are useful for more advanced riders, as well as information about brake hardware and how it can influence your connection with brake feel. The final section provides practice drills to help you develop braking confidence.

The purpose of this chapter is to give you the tools to manage roadway challenges and to avoid collisions. Utilizing this information will give you the ability to slow and stop with precision at a moment's notice. When braking skill becomes second nature, confidence increases and you are able to devote more attention to managing potential hazards and tuning into your surroundings.

developing brake feel

To brake effectively you must develop a feel for how much braking power is available without losing control. Brake feel is a learned skill that requires you to develop a sense for how your motorcycle's brakes respond to subtle inputs. An acute sense of brake feel allows you to calibrate your mind, fingers, and foot to brake with precision. Once you develop this skill you can sense slight fluctuations in traction levels and fine-tune brake pressure to adjust speed with accuracy and maintain control.

Your senses play a key role in determining available braking power. Your brain senses the rate of deceleration by interpreting information it receives through receptors in your muscles and inner ear, as well as the visual data transmitted through your eyes. Your brain also receives information from your tires, suspension, and brake hardware through the nerves in your fingers as they squeeze the brake lever and through your right foot as it presses the rear brake pedal. These nerves allow you to sense resistance and friction levels between the brake pads and rotors, and between the tires and road. This feedback helps you determine whether lever or pedal pressure must be adjusted to achieve the desired braking results.

Extreme brake force can cause a sportbike to stand on its nose.

To develop brake feel you must understand the effect of braking force on traction and over-all control. Squeezing the front brake lever or pressing on the rear brake pedal slows the motorcycle, but it also causes the bike to pitch forward, which changes the amount of traction available at each tire. This is significant because the amount of traction you have directly influences how much brake pressure you can use. (See Chapter 6 for information on traction and load.)

A dramatic result of strong or excessive brake force is when the rear wheel lifts off the pavement completely—a "stoppie." Stoppies are more likely when riding a sport bike that typically has a high Center of Gravity (CG) in relation to its wheelbase.

avoid skids

Many motorcyclists mistakenly believe that a skidding tire provides equal or better stopping friction than a rolling tire. In reality, friction diminishes once a tire begins to slide.

You can feel this by placing your palm on a table surface and pressing down just enough to keep your hand stationary while trying to slide it forward. This is called "static friction." Now, exert more sliding force to overcome the downward load that is keeping your hand in place. Notice that once your hand begins to slide, it slides very quickly. This "sliding friction" is less than static friction, and shows what happens when tires skid as you overcome static friction.

Also, when tires skid, heat builds up, further reducing friction. The result is a tire that slides uncontrollably. The trick to maintaining control while braking hard is to first understand the capability and limitations of each brake and then practice to develop a feel for how hard you can apply the brakes before a skid occurs.

engine braking

Engine braking is often used to slow a motorcycle, but it's important to recognize that engine braking has the same effect as rear wheel braking. While it's common and acceptable to use engine braking for small reductions in speed, you will need to use your brakes for significant speed adjustments. Also, be aware that extreme engine braking can cause rear tire skids, especially on high torque V-twin motorcycles. (See Chapter 10 for more on shifting.)

↘ on your next ride

Familiarize yourself with the characteristics of your brakes by noticing subtle sensations transmitted from both the front and rear brakes.

Sense the brake pads as they rub on the brake discs.

Notice how brake power varies with brake pressure.

Does brake power increase progressively or evenly with increased lever pressure?

Does brake power come on quickly or slowly?

Notice how rear brake force reduces forward dive.

Observe that using the rear brake alone requires more pressure to slow the motorcycle.

Give the brake pedal a very firm press to cause a skid. Do this at a slow speed and while straight up and down to avoid a fall. This can give you valuable insight about how much pressure you can apply before you lock the tire.

Being sharply aware of these traits will help your brain and nerves become familiar with your motorcycle's brake characteristics. With the ability to sense how your brakes will respond you can modulate brake force to a very fine level. The visceral feedback you receive will tell you whether you can brake harder without skidding and opens a special connection between you and your motorcycle that significantly increases confidence and enjoyment.

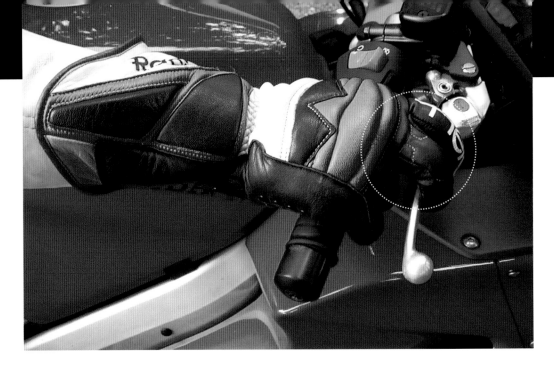

master the front brake

The front brake is the most important tool for stopping quickly, but using the front brake with confidence can be difficult to master. You might shy away from the front brake if you have ever experienced a previous fall due to overuse of the front brake, or because you are simply accustomed to braking with your foot as you do when driving a car.

The front brake is the primary means for stopping because forward load transfer increases front tire traction. You feel this force as you are thrust forward every time you use the brakes in a car or on a bike. To take advantage of the large amount of front tire traction, most motorcycles are equipped with large, powerful front brakes.

It's important to understand that you can lock the front tire if you apply brake power before the tire is adequately loaded. To avoid a skid, squeeze the brake lever progressively to allow tire load and traction to increase before introducing more brake force.

This is why it is important that you train yourself *never to grab* the front brake suddenly. Instead, *squeeze the front brake firmly and progressively* to allow traction levels to rise. Once sufficient load is transferred to the front tire you can *squeeze harder.*

1 *Squeeze to load the suspension and front tire.*   **2** *Squeeze harder.*

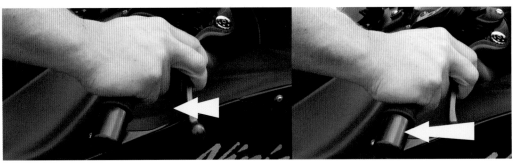

understand the rear brake

Even though the front brake is the most important brake to master because it controls the greater braking force, the rear brake is useful for shortening stopping distances and for helping to stabilize the motorcycle.

Uninformed riders rely mostly on the rear brake, even though it provides less braking force than the front brake. Perhaps this is because of car driving habits or because of the largely unfounded fear of flipping over the handlebars. As an MSF Experienced RiderCourse® instructor, I have observed hundreds of seasoned riders with this bad habit. It takes several attempts to prove the benefit of reversing their brake use to favor the front brake. Eventually they learn to trust the front brake and their stopping distances shorten significantly.

One thing that students inevitably discover is that applying more front brake force increases the likelihood of rear tire skids, because forward load transfer decreases load, and therefore traction, at the rear tire. Because of this, some riders avoid the rear brake altogether. However, not using the rear brake means you're not taking advantage of its extra stopping power and the increased stability it offers.

It takes practice to use the front brake to its potential and modulate the rear brake to avoid a rear tire skid. The trick is to reduce rear brake pressure as load shifts forward just enough to keep the rear tire rolling.

There are times when it's best to use the rear brake only, such as when riding on very slippery or loose surfaces where the front brake can be too powerful. In these conditions, rear brake power is much more controllable and an inadvertent rear tire skid is much more controllable compared to a front tire skid.

The rear brake has a more important role when stopping in low traction situations for another reason. Naturally, you shouldn't brake as hard in wet conditions due to minimal traction, which means that there will be less forward load transfer and more weight will remain over the rear tire for more rear brake traction.

The rear brake also helps stabilize the bike when stopping or slowing. To minimize forward pitch, apply the rear brake a moment before progressively squeezing the front brake. This technique allows the whole bike to "squat" for a more level attitude. The rear brake also enhances stability by essentially "pulling" the center of gravity and the rear of the motorcycle in line with the front wheel and the direction of travel. Note that you can benefit from this same stabilizing force with engine braking.

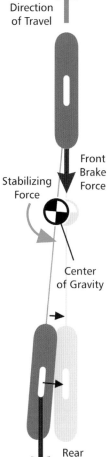

Direction of Travel

Stabilizing Force

Front Brake Force

Center of Gravity

Rear Brake Force

↘ laying it down

There was a time—in the distant past—when motorcycle brakes and tires didn't perform very well, which led to a stopping technique known as "laying it down." With today's brake and tire technology, it is possible for a skilled rider to stop a motorcycle in much shorter distances than in the past. So, rather than tossing your motorcycle on its side, it's better to keep your motorcycle upright and brake hard to avoid a hazard.

emergency braking

Being skilled enough to stop your motorcycle in the shortest possible distance can literally save your life. Unfortunately, too many riders lack the ability to stop their motorcycle quickly without error. They either overbrake, underbrake, or use the wrong brake.

To stop a motorcycle quickly you must use all of the means available to you, which means applying both brakes to their maximum without skidding. To do this requires knowledge and practice. It's important to keep this skill sharp, because you will perform according to whatever habits you have. Well-practiced braking skills will allow you to perform a maximum stop while remaining in control, even if the circumstances seem dire.

Braking in the shortest possible distance means braking to the point of impending skid. As I said earlier, it's important to squeeze the brake lever progressively to avoid skidding the front tire. If you grab the front brake quickly, you will introduce too much brake power onto a front tire that is not yet loaded and a skid may occur.

There is a limit to how much brake power you can use. Even if the front tire is fully loaded a skid can occur if braking force exceeds available traction. Fortunately, today's tires offer excellent grip, which makes it possible to apply a very high level of braking force to a front tire on clean, dry pavement, as long as you squeeze the brake progressively. To prevent a rear tire skid, you must gradually reduce rear brake force as the weight transfers forward.

Road surface condition has a lot to do with how much braking force you can apply. Avoid crack sealer, sandy pavement, and other contaminated surfaces so that you have maximum traction available if you need to brake.

The distance it takes to perform an emergency stop is also affected by perception and reaction time. It takes a significant amount of time and distance for a rider to react as the brain comprehends a dangerous situation unfolding. Smart riders reduce perception time and reaction time by predicting potential problems well in advance and increasing readiness by covering their brakes.

emergency corner braking

Sometimes you need to stop quickly while leaned in a turn. An untrained rider typically responds with a knee-jerk grab of the brakes, followed shortly by the sickening sound of scraping metal and plastic. To perform a quick stop from a lean, you must manage the limited amount of traction available. (See the Traction Circles in Chapter 6.)

A quick stop in a curve can be performed in two ways:

1. **Straighten the bike** (by quickly pressing on the outside handgrip) to make more traction available for braking, then apply maximum brake power in a straight-line. This option is not always possible if straightening means running off the road or colliding with an oncoming car in the opposite lane. In this case, use option #2.

1 Straighten, then brake

2. **Brake while leaned** by applying as much brake power as possible without losing traction and using more brake pressure as the motorcycle slows and straightens. This is one situation where your ability to feel the brakes will pay off big time (see Braking Drill #5).

2 Brake carefully while leaned; brake harder as the bike straightens.

↘ avoid braking while swerving

Swerving is essentially two consecutive turns; one to avoid an obstacle, the second to get back on track. This means that there is little braking traction available when swerving, so you must separate braking from swerving. If you must brake and swerve, release the brakes before swerving, then apply the brakes again once you are upright.

brake timing and intensity

The ability to brake with accurate control and precise timing is a cornerstone to skillful riding. You feel immense satisfaction when you can apply the brakes with just the right amount of pressure and at the exact moment to slow for a complex turn or to stop smoothly. This precision contributes greatly to a feeling of mastery and confidence.

Well-timed braking is critical for maintaining traction and control. If you wait too long to apply the brakes before stopping at an intersection, you'll have to brake hard, possibly causing the tires to slide on slick road markings or accumulated fluids from idling vehicles.

Skillful brake timing is also necessary for safe cornering. One of the most common errors is to delay braking until the last moment. "Charging" into corners not only increases the likelihood of panic it also increases instability as you compress the necessary braking into a shorter amount of time and distance. Make it your general practice to enter corners slower than necessary. You can always roll on the throttle if you slowed too much, but correcting an entry that is too fast is more difficult.

A feeling of being rushed before a corner is often caused by braking too late, but it can also be the result of too little brake pressure (intensity). If you feel rushed because you have too little time to release the brakes before turning the motorcycle, either brake sooner or increase brake pressure. Either way, you'll reach your desired entry speed earlier, which results in a more controlled, relaxed corner entry.

Imagine two riders entering the same corner moments apart, at about the same speed. Rider #1 brakes firmly, yet smoothly, keeping his bike stable and in line as he fluidly slows for the turn. Rider #2 delays braking by 20 feet and instead of smoothly applying the brakes he jabs them abruptly, causing his motorcycle to wag from side to side. Isn't it obvious which rider has better control?

trail braking

To ensure the greatest traction and safety, it's best to complete all of your braking before leaning into a corner. However, there are times when braking past the turn-in point is desirable or necessary.

Trail braking is the act of braking while leaning into a turn, then gradually releasing ("trailing") the brakes as lean angle increases until there is zero brake pressure at full lean. This is usually a planned maneuver and is most appropriate for racers who use this braking technique to quicken turn-in, stabilize the motorcycle when transitioning from braking to lean, and to keep the competition at bay.

We discussed in Chapter 6 that traction for braking is limited when cornering, therefore, braking while in a lean is risky and requires a high level of control to avoid sliding your tires. Trail braking is not recommended for typical street riding situations. Unlike on a racetrack, the street holds no guarantees that the next turn is what you expect, that the corner is clean, or the road clear.

Even though street riders are normally better off not trail braking, the ability to trail brake can be very useful. Having the ability to slow while you are leaned can salvage a too-fast entry speed, or help you avoid an obstacle that appears just as you are leaning the bike.

Trail braking can also be used to tighten a mid-corner path. This is done using only the rear brake and is often a better choice than introducing handlebar inputs at maximum lean, an action that can cause the front tire to lose traction and "tuck." Carefully modulate rear brake pressure to prevent sliding the rear tire.

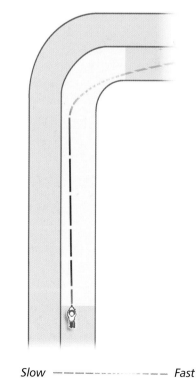

Slow – – – – – – – – – – *Fast*

ease on, ease off

Earlier, I talked about the importance of applying the brakes progressively. Not only does this allow time for the front tire to increase traction, it also minimizes forward pitch or dive that can upset your motorcycle's stability.

It's also important to *release* the brakes smoothly in order to avoid abrupt rebounding of the front fork springs, which can cause the front tire to unload and possibly lose traction. This is especially likely when cornering. Even if you don't lose traction, the extended forks can push the bike into a wider line than desired.

how many fingers?

Most modern brake systems deliver impressive stopping power, even with two-finger front brake operation. However, vintage bikes and some heavy touring bikes and cruisers that have relatively weak and inefficient front brakes will require four-finger braking to stop quickly.

The advantage of two-finger braking is that it allows the two remaining digits to remain on the throttle grip (usually the ring finger and pinkie). This is useful when implementing advanced throttle/brake techniques such as brake and throttle overlapping or throttle blipping (see Chapter 10). Two-finger braking can also help with precise modulation; however, some riders believe that four-finger braking offers better feel because more nerve sensors are in contact with the front brake lever. It's not important whether you use two, three, or four fingers to brake; what is important is that you discover the best combination of power, feedback, and control for maximum braking.

Determine the optimum number of fingers to use then use that combination *all the time,* because in an emergency you'll fall back on whatever habits you've developed. Attempting to apply the precise amount of maximum brake pressure using four fingers after habitually braking with two fingers isn't realistic. While it's possible to use both two- and four-finger techniques, it's better for most riders to master one technique and stick with it.

↘ overlap technique

For additional control, use the throttle/brake overlap technique: begin throttle roll-on just before completely releasing the brakes to smooth the transition from braking force to driving force.

The brake/throttle overlap technique takes some practice. One helpful technique is to curl your fingers over the front brake lever as you squeeze, then simply straighten your fingers to release brake pressure as you roll on the throttle. (See Braking Drill #1 at the end of the chapter.)

brake character

Every motorcycle provides its own unique amount and quality of brake feel depending on the brake system design, maintenance, brake pad compound, and tire construction.

Some brake systems provide excellent feedback, delivering visceral information in the form of vibration and tactile resistance as your fingertips squeeze the brake lever, or your foot presses the brake pedal. Systems with the most feedback allow you to feel the texture of the brake pad material and rotor surface as they slide against each other and allow you to sense exactly how the brakes will respond to a given amount of brake pressure. This feedback is very helpful for developing maximum braking confidence.

Not all brake systems deliver clear tactile messages. Some systems deliver a smooth feel with little vibration or visceral information. These brakes are often described as "wooden," providing little tactile feedback about how the brakes are performing. You may question whether the brakes will respond smoothly or abruptly or if they will provide the expected amount of power at the right time. It is possible to become accustomed to a lack of brake feedback, but it is difficult to put full confidence in a system that feels vague. Sometimes a different type of brake pad or braided steel brake lines can remedy this condition.

Brake systems also vary in how evenly they deliver brake power. Some have linear power delivery, while others get progressively stronger as the brake lever is squeezed. Linear power delivery is often more predictable. Progressive brakes need a bit more care to achieve just the right amount of brake power.

Brake lever, caliper, and master cylinder design each contribute to power and feel. The latest motorcycles come with radial-mounted brake calipers and master cylinders that minimize flex for superior power and direct feedback.

Tire construction also plays a role in brake feedback. A tire with stiff sidewalls will flex less than a tire with a more compliant sidewall. The stiffer tire can transfer subtle information about traction somewhat better than a more flexible carcass, which can muffle feedback about grip level.

brake problems

Extreme operating conditions and neglected maintenance can contribute to poor feedback and a lack of braking efficiency. One such condition is a "spongy" feeling when you squeeze the brake lever. This is often caused by air being trapped in the system. The usual solution is to bleed the brakes carefully to ensure that no air is trapped in the fluid. Brake bleeding is a project easily handled by those who are mechanically inclined, but can be a fussy procedure. If you are not familiar with brake bleeding procedure, you may want to ask another experienced rider to walk you through it.

Another condition is brake "fade," a condition usually caused by extreme overheating of the brakes. This can result from repeated hard braking from high speeds, or from continual braking on long downhill runs.

One more undesirable condition is when the brakes just don't seem to have much "bite." The cause may be from brake system design or it may be that the brake pads have become glazed from improper run-in or overheating and need to be replaced.

If you experience brake fade or insufficient bite even after careful maintenance, consider choosing high-performance brake fluid and brake pads designed for maximum feedback and extreme conditions. Braided steel or Kevlar brake lines can improve brake feel and high-performance brake pads can increase heat resistance. Note that race-compound brake pads are designed to perform best at high temperatures and may not be appropriate for the wide range of conditions typical of street riding.

brake adjustments

Becoming "one" with your motorcycle requires exceptional control of your brakes. Adjust your front brake lever and rear brake pedal for the best feel and precision. You can achieve optimum front brake control by adjusting the lever to a position that allows your forearm and wrist to be flat when applying the brake. You may be able to adjust the distance of the lever from the handlebar by turning the dial found on many modern brake levers.

Rear brake pedals are also adjustable. Many have screw adjusters, but some may require removing the pedal and repositioning it onto the splined shaft at a different location. Note that you may need to adjust your rear brake light switch as well.

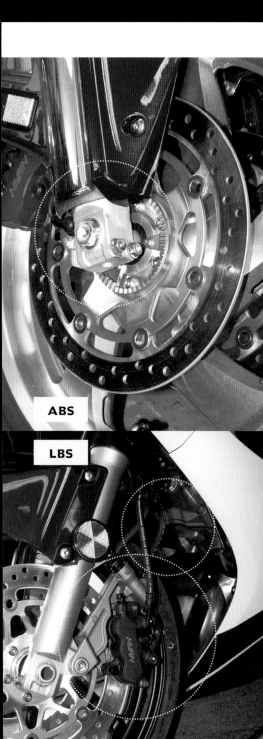

ABS

LBS

↘ brake systems

More and more motorcycles come equipped with non-standard brake systems, so it's important to understand their features and benefits so you can use them to their full potential.

Anti-lock braking systems (ABS) use electronics to release brake pressure in rapid pulses after sensing interruptions in wheel speed (skidding).

ABS prevents skids, which translates into shorter stopping distances on slippery surfaces and increased rider confidence. ABS increases control when braking in a straight line, but ABS can't do much to prevent a slide-out when cornering, because the system detects only whether the wheel is spinning slower or faster, not whether the tire is sliding sideways.

Linked braking systems (LBS) consist of complex hydraulic plumbing that activates both the front and rear calipers. Only when both the front brake lever and the rear brake pedal are applied will full brake power be realized.

Integrated braking systems have both front and rear brakes controlled together, often with a proportioning valve that favors the front brake.

The advantage of linked and integrated brake systems is to ensure application of both front and rear brakes in an emergency situation when an untrained rider might stomp on the rear brake pedal while ignoring the front brake lever or vice versa.

It's important to note that linked and integrated systems make it impossible to use rear-brake-only techniques that are useful in low traction situations, such as braking on loose surfaces or controlling speed in slow U-turns by dragging the rear brake.

braking practice

It's important to keep your braking skills sharp, because your response to an emergency situation is highly conditioned by whatever habits you have. Continual practice puts this information into your muscle memory so you will respond properly when you need to. (See the braking drills that follow.)

A parking lot session consisting of several maximum braking stops will give you valuable experience to learn how your bike feels under extreme braking. To prevent a fall always brake with progressive pressure and avoid grabbing and stomping. And wear full protective gear, just in case.

Practicing emergency braking will not only help you acquire a life-saving skill, it can also give you greater knowledge and respect for your motorcycle's braking potential. That, in turn, leads to greater confidence and comfort with your motorcycle.

braking drills

To minimize the risk of injury, wear full protective gear whenever you ride.

braking drill #1 - smooth braking transitions

BENEFITS

- Learn to minimize chassis pitch when braking
- Refine brake and throttle transitions (see page 82)

SETUP

- An area where you can ride back and forth and brake in a straight line (about 150 feet long)

INSTRUCTIONS

1 From a speed of about 25 to 30 mph reduce speed by smoothly and progressively applying the front brake only (do not come to a full stop).
2 Release the brake and roll on the throttle as seamlessly as possible.
3 Continue to practice smoothly squeezing and releasing the front brake.

NOTES

- Curl your fingers over the front brake lever when squeezing the lever.
- Straighten your fingers to release brake pressure as you smoothly roll on the throttle.
- For the smoothest transitions use your index and middle fingers to squeeze the brake lever and your ring and pinkie fingers to control the throttle.
- Notice how applying and releasing the brake progressively causes the front forks to compress and rebound smoothly.

braking drill #2 - straight-line braking

BENEFITS

- Increase brake control
- Learn and sense your motorcycle's braking potential
- Understand the role each brake has on stability

SETUP

You will need an area where you can ride back and forth and brake in a straight line (about 150 feet long). If you want to measure stopping distances you will need a mark where you will begin braking and a second mark set at about 35 feet. Strive to stop within 35 feet from 30 mph.

INSTRUCTIONS

For each part, approach the braking area at about 25 mph in second gear. At the "begin braking" mark apply the brakes, squeeze the clutch, and downshift to first gear. Keep the clutch squeezed as you come to a stop. Do not use engine braking.

PART 1 - FRONT BRAKE ONLY

- Notice the amount of brake lever force that is required and the amount of forward load transfer you experience (see pages 64–65).

PART 2 - REAR BRAKE ONLY

- Notice the difference in forward load transfer, compared with using the front brake. Also notice how hard you must press the brake pedal to stop. If you want, give the brake pedal a very firm press to cause a skid. (To avoid a fall do this at no more than 20 mph and while straight up and down.)

PART 3 - BOTH BRAKES

- Notice shorter stopping distance and a slight increase in stability.

PART 4 - REAR BRAKE FIRST

- Apply the rear brake one second before the front brake.
- Notice the stabilizing effect of the rear brake. This effect is more noticeable on bikes with softer suspension (see page 77).

PART 5 - PRACTICE EMERGENCY STOPS

- Continue to practice braking with the goal of stopping in a shorter and shorter distance.
- Apply progressive pressure.
- Ease off the rear brake as weight transfers forward to prevent a rear tire skid.

braking drill #3 - corner braking

PARKING LOT SETUP

An area where you can ride in a circle about 100 feet in diameter (approximately the width of 10 parking spaces)

BENEFITS

- ◆ Increase confidence when braking while leaned
- ◆ Increase understanding of traction while braking in corners
- ◆ Increase understanding of how brake force affects cornering direction and lean angle.

INSTRUCTIONS

1 Ride around the circle to the left in second gear at about 25 mph.
2 Roll off the throttle while *smoothly and lightly* applying both brakes.
3 Downshift (without releasing the clutch) and come to a stop.
4 Repeat to the right.

Notice how your motorcycle responds to mid-corner braking; it may "stand up" or it may lean more. You may notice that slower or higher speeds affect it differently. It's important to relax your arms to feel the effect mid-corner braking has on your bike.

NOTE: You must be gentle when braking in corners to prevent a skid.

braking drill #4 - trail braking

PARKING LOT SETUP
An area where you can ride in a circle
about 100 feet in diameter
(approximately the width of 10 parking spaces)

BENEFITS
- Develop a fundamental understanding and feel for braking into a turn while remaining in control
- Minimize fear of braking in a curve

INSTRUCTIONS
1. Approach the circle straight at about 30 mph.
2. Brake smoothly yet firmly as you enter the curve.
3. Continue braking as you lean into the curve.
4. Ease off the brakes completely before you are fully leaned.
5. Roll on the throttle smoothly.

NOTE: You must be gentle when braking in corners to prevent a skid, but firm enough to feel the effect.

8

Cornering is arguably the most enjoyable aspect of motorcycling. After all, not much can match the feel of leaning into a turn, the cornering forces pressing you into the motorcycle's seat and creating the sensation that you are somehow defying gravity. Skillfully stringing together a series of corners can make you feel like a master.

Part of the reason cornering is so much fun is that it's challenging. Unfortunately, the majority of single-vehicle crashes involve riders who were unable to negotiate a corner successfully; they either didn't foresee a mid-corner hazard or didn't have the confidence or skill to make the turn. When a corner turns more sharply than expected, a rider who lacks cornering confidence easily panics, and may respond by rolling off the throttle, stabbing the brakes, and fixing his eyes on the outside of the turn. This usually results in broken bodywork, or worse.

In this chapter, you'll learn exactly how to turn your motorcycle. This knowledge alone will help to increase your confidence and enjoyment of cornering, but there is more to safe and enjoyable cornering than simply getting your motorcycle to turn. It's important to implement a "cornering plan" for each and every corner you ride, to reduce the likelihood that you will encounter surprises. In addition, strengthening your cornering skills will let you approach corners with greater confidence and precision.

Lean to Turn

The simple fact is that motorcycles must lean to turn. However, many riders struggle with turning because they don't understand the best way to initiate lean. For them, cornering is a source of tension rather than enjoyment. Once you understand and practice exactly *how* to get your motorcycle to turn efficiently, your riding can reach a whole new level of enjoyment.

countersteering

Achieving confidence in cornering begins by mastering the simple, yet confusing, technique called *countersteering*. It isn't necessary to understand the science to put the technique to use. All you really need to know is that handlebar inputs are the primary means to lean your motorcycle: you push on the handgrip on the side toward which you want to turn; push left to go left and push right to go right.

You're not alone if countersteering confuses you; after all, pressing on the right handlebar (which turns the handlebars slightly left) to go right and vice versa just seems wrong. But, it's true. You may not have noticed it, but if you've ridden a motorcycle before—or a bicycle for that matter—you've used countersteering.

A very basic explanation of how countersteering works may help. By pressing lightly and momentarily on the right handlebar you steer the front wheel to the left, causing the tire's contact patch to move off-center, to the left. This leftward "out-tracking" motion of the tire's contact patch upsets the upright balance of the motorcycle, causing it to "fall over" to the right, into a lean. Countersteering is assisted by gyroscopic forces of the spinning wheels to force the motorcycle into a lean.

3 *The rider releases pressure and steers to maintain balance.*

2 *...which causes the motorcycle to lean right.*

1 *Rider pushes on the right handlebar, turning the front wheel left...*

↘ press forward or press down?

Countersteering requires the rider to "steer" the front tire out from underneath the motorcycle, which is best accomplished by turning the handlebars. Sit on a stationary motorcycle and turn the handlebars left and right. Does pressing forward or down cause the front wheel to turn more easily? This experiment should convince you that a forward push is most efficient.

In reality, though, most riders push forward and down. This is partly because your arm's angle to the handlebars is far from perpendicular to the steering pivot, which means that unless you hunker down like a racer you will be putting a good portion of the force in a downward direction when pressing the handlebar. Of course, the angle of force will vary from bike to bike depending on handlebar height.

countersteering refinement

Once you have mastered the basic countersteering technique you can begin to explore ways to refine your turning skills, giving you more control and transforming uncertainty into genuine cornering confidence.

* For maximum countersteering efficiency direct your arm motion primarily forward, not down.
* Avoid unconsciously pressing forward on *both* handlebars. This is often the cause of turning difficulties, because pressing both handlebars forward cancels out the effectiveness of countersteering.
* Relax your arms once you have achieved the desired lean angle, to let the motorcycle track through the turn.
* When the road turns a bit tighter than anticipated, lean further by pressing harder on the inside grip (see Cornering Drill #1).
* For quicker turns that require more handlebar force you can assist the countersteering press by *pulling* on the opposite handlebar; for example, pull on the right handlebar to go left and vice versa.

Handlebar width, as well as fork angle, affects steering leverage.

⬓ how much pressure?

The amount of lean angle required is determined by the relationship between corner speed and the turn radius. A turn ridden at 40 mph speed requires greater lean angle than the same turn ridden at 30 mph. Press on the handlebar with the correct amount of force and duration to attain the lean angle necessary for the turn. Reduce pressure as the motorcycle reaches the desired lean.

In most cornering situations, the countersteering action will feel like a smooth, progressive motion with very slight, almost imperceptible levels of handlebar pressure. However, some corners require a more rapid turn-in. To cause your motorcycle to lean quickly, press more forcefully.

The amount of pressure you'll need to apply to the handlebar also depends on the weight of your motorcycle, as well as its handlebar width, height and angle, tire profile, and steering geometry. For instance, wide, tall bars provide greater leverage. A steep steering geometry will likewise make turn-in easier compared to a "raked out" front end.

Pay close attention to the amount of handlebar pressure needed for different types of corners. Recognize that some turns require gentle pressure, while others require more force for quicker turning. Over time, you will develop an intimate sensitivity for exactly how much countersteering effort is needed to corner with precision.

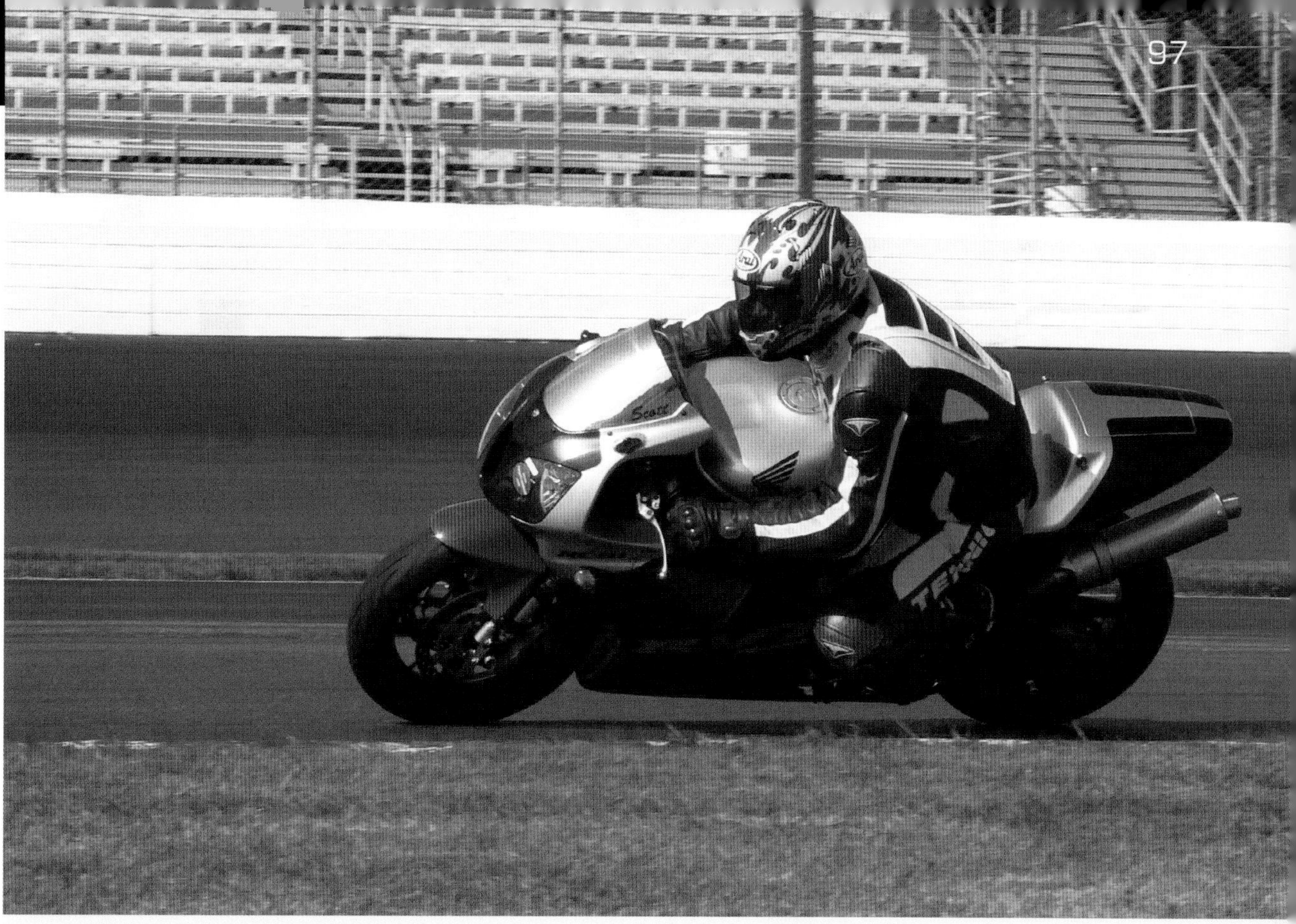

the physics of cornering

The cornering process involves more than just initiating lean. Once the motorcycle is leaned other forces take over to allow it to carve an arc. Centripetal force (commonly mistaken for centrifugal force) keeps the bike leaning toward the center of the curve as the inertia of the motorcycle/rider mass attempts to return to a straight-ahead path. Additionally, the conical shape of motorcycle tires causes the wheels to carve a sharper arc when leaned as the smaller diameter outer edge of the tire comes in contact with the road.

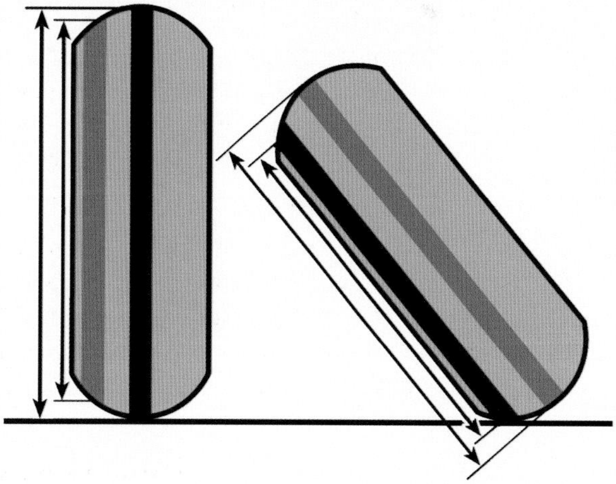

The contact ring is located off-center when the motorcycle is leaned.

The laws of physics have conspired in wondrous ways to balance all these forces so that all you have to do is initiate lean and your motorcycle corners with ease. Learning to control your motorcycle's dynamics with precision leads to confidence and satisfaction.

make a cornering plan

Now that you have an understanding of how your motorcycle turns, let's talk about developing "cornering plans" to help you make good decisions that allow you to negotiate any corner with precision and safety. A cornering plan is needed for each and every corner you come upon.

A CORNERING PLAN IS BASED ON

- **Corner locations,** which include the approach, entry, apex, and exit locations
- **Corner characteristics,** such as corner radius, road camber, slope, pavement condition, and surface texture
- **Cornering lines** that straighten the path and set you up for the next turn

corner locations

A Cornering Plan begins by understanding the four general locations where cornering actions occur: the approach, the entry, the apex, and the exit locations.

The **approach** location is where you make decisions regarding entry speed and where you begin to turn. Look well ahead for clues about what type of turn you are about to encounter, then determine where you will roll off the throttle, apply the brakes, and turn-in. At this point, you will also determine an appropriate cornering line.

The **entry** location is where you initiate lean to turn. Exactly where the entry is located depends on corner radius, how quickly and forcefully you countersteer, and your chosen cornering line. Begin gentle acceleration immediately after turn-in.

The **apex** location is the point along the inside edge and near the center of a corner's arc. The exact location of the apex varies with the type of radius and where you need to exit. A delayed apex offers a better angle of view into the turn while adding a measure of protection from running wide at the exit if done correctly. If the corner exit is the entrance to another corner in a series, your apex location may need to be adjusted to allow for a proper entry location for the next turn. I'll discuss cornering lines more fully later.

The **exit** location is where you accelerate to complete the corner. The exit location of a single turn will be located toward the outside of the turn. But on a twisty road the exit from one turn may well be the entrance for the next turn, so select an exit that will set you up for the next curve.

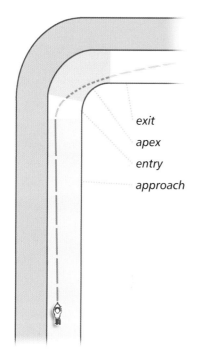

exit

apex

entry

approach

Riding with confidence means responding assertively and skillfully to anything the environment throws at you. Having a plan for knowing when, where, and how to manage each corner's unique characteristics greatly increases cornering confidence and satisfaction.

corner characteristics

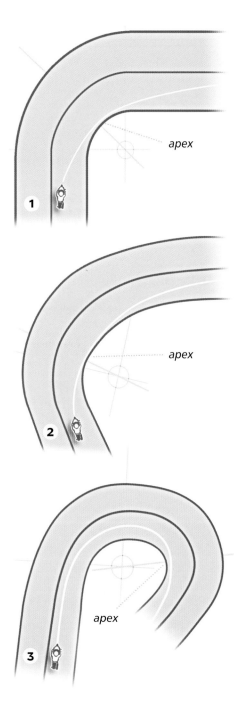

Awareness of corner features, such as radius, camber, and surface condition, combined with knowledge about how to handle them, reduces anxiety and gives you confidence that you can manage any turn. Evaluate the characteristics of each corner to help create your cornering plan.

corner radius

1   **Constant-radius** turns resemble a section of a circle with a constant arc from beginning to end. The apex of constant-radius turns is located about halfway between the entry and the exit. A constant angle of lean is used. This type of corner is the least complicated or scary.

2   **Increasing-radius** turns begin with a tighter radius then gradually straighten out. Increasing-radius turns inspire confidence, because they "open up" toward the exit. The apex is located earlier in the corner than a constant-radius turn. Typically, you will turn and accelerate earlier compared to a constant-radius turn.

3   **Decreasing-radius** turns are the most challenging type of corner, because they tighten as you proceed from corner entry to the exit. Decreasing-radius turns require much slower entry speeds, because an increasing lean angle is required as you proceed toward the exit. Decreasing-radius turns can change by varying amounts; some turns tighten up significantly, while others tighten up only a small amount. The safest apex is located farther around the corner from the halfway point, possibly very near the exit. Decreasing-radius turns can appear anywhere, but are most commonly encountered on highway entrance and exit ramps.

These three corner types will appear on every ride you take. You may even encounter each of the three types within a single series of corners.

Look well ahead to identify the next corner's radius to determine the best course of action. For instance, if the first corner empties into a decreasing-radius turn you must exit the first corner at a slower speed so you are prepared to handle the more difficult corner.

It's not always possible to determine the exact radius of an upcoming corner. Sometimes you can determine the turn radius by looking at treetops or power lines, but they don't always mirror the curve of the road. One way to determine where a road is headed is to observe whether the white fog lines on either side of the road or the road edges themselves are visually merging in the near distance. An even better tack is to choose conservative entry speeds whenever the corner is obscured.

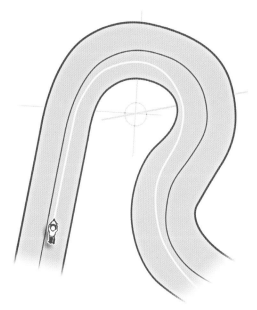

surface camber and slope

Roadway pitch, camber, and elevation are significant corner characteristics to be aware of. *Camber* refers to the side-to-side slope of the road surface. Most roads have a "crowned" camber for draining water from the center to the road shoulders, which means that ground clearance for a leaning motorcycle is reduced when turning left, but is increased when turning right.

Well-engineered corners have their surface "banked" with the outside of the turn higher than the inside to improve road holding. Unfortunately, some roads slope in the wrong direction. These "off camber" (or "negative camber") turns challenge available traction as gravity and cornering forces require the tires to work harder to prevent sliding down the road's slope. To prevent traction loss in off-camber turns, it's important to slow down to reduce cornering forces and look well ahead to determine the ideal line for maximum ground clearance and grip.

Uphill and downhill sloping sections can also add a level of complexity to cornering. Plan ahead and reduce speed for downhill corners; downshift for adequate power on uphill corners . Also, downhill corners put extra stress on the front tire, increasing the risk of a front tire slide. Slow more before downhill corners so you can roll on the throttle to relieve front tire stress. Uphill turns unload the front tire, resulting in less grip for turning. In this situation, it's best to accelerate carefully to keep the front tire planted.

pavement condition and texture

The third characteristic to evaluate is the quality of the road surface. Look for moisture, debris, or surface irregularities to determine whether adequate traction is available.

I pointed out in Chapter 6 that traction quality varies with surface texture. A smooth texture offers less grip and often has a glossy look as light reflects off its shiny surface. Some examples of smooth surfaces include metal construction plates, manhole covers, tar crack filler, and very worn pavement. Textured surfaces provide superior grip and often have a dull appearance.

Identifying surface traction quality is more difficult if the road is coated with water. Rainwater reduces traction by lubricating the surface, but only cuts traction by perhaps 20% to 30% if the road surface is good when dry. However, water on top of an already slick area will only make it more slippery. Of course you must avoid very slippery contaminants, such as anti-freeze, motor oil, or diesel fuel, because they greatly increase the chances for a slide.

Cornering Lines

One facet of your cornering plan is the cornering line, or path through the curve. Riding a narrow, single-track vehicle allows you to select multiple lane positions—left, center, or right—allowing you to use the full width of your lane in negotiating curves. Many riders don't think about cornering lines, but as you will see, they aren't taking advantage of a very useful concept.

The basic cornering line is an **outside-inside-outside** path. The obvious advantage of this path is that it straightens the corner by carving a larger radius, thereby preserving traction reserve. Another advantage is the increased angle of sight through the curve that allows you to spot mid-corner hazards early and to identify corner characteristics.

Be careful not to ride too closely to the centerline in left-hand turns to avoid leaning into the oncoming lane or risking hitting a roadside obstacle by riding too close to the road's edge in right-hand turns.

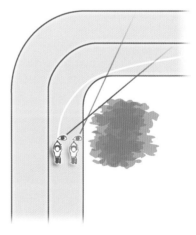

The "outside-inside-outside" cornering line straightens the curve and improves line of sight.

One variation on the basic cornering line is the **delayed-apex** line. This path starts from the outside of the curve just like the basic cornering line, but the apex is located farther around the corner. Stay outside and delay turn-in for the best angle of view and to point your bike toward the exit. Exercise caution with delayed-apex lines; waiting too long to turn can cause you to run wide.

Using cornering lines contributes to your confidence by minimizing lean angle and increasing sight distance. Using cornering lines in everyday riding also puts you in harmony with each corner you encounter. Reading each turn and executing a smooth, precise line is a true expression of cornering mastery.

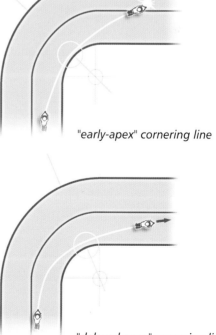

"early-apex" cornering line

"delayed-apex" cornering line

cornering actions

Now that we've identified cornering locations, evaluated which corner characteristics deserve attention, and talked about cornering lines it's time to discuss in detail the physical actions necessary to execute corners successfully.

Cornering involves four basic actions:

- Adjust entry speed
- Look through the turn
- Initiate lean
- Accelerate through the turn

adjust entry speed

The first step of the cornering sequence is to adjust your entry speed. A suitable entry speed is determined by corner characteristics and surface conditions, as well as your cornering ability. A comfortable entry speed is crucial to avert the cornering anxiety and panic that may lead to a crash.

Speed adjustment should be made at the corner's approach location, usually requiring deceleration and braking. Many corners require significant speed reduction with firm brake pressure and perhaps a downshift or two. This is common when a tight turn appears at the end of a straight or when you accelerate significantly between curves. Not every corner requires considerable speed adjustments, as when you are riding at moderate speeds through a series of gentle curves. However, it is important to recognize that you must evaluate every corner to determine an appropriate entry speed and whether you must slow significantly or not.

Earlier, I mentioned how the "panic test" can help determine your comfort level. If you feel tension or a twinge of panic when cornering, then you can be sure that you're entering turns too fast. To help determine proper entry speeds, evaluate your comfort level and honestly assess your limits. It takes a concerted effort to maintain a high level of self-awareness. Reduce the likelihood of poor judgement by avoiding over-confidence, inattention, or impairment.

⟍ slow in, fast out

Many riders who strive to go faster through turns make the mistake of "rushing" into corners by delaying speed adjustment until the last possible moment. This approach offers no real benefit and usually results in heightened anxiety. To minimize risk and stress, get into the habit of slowing earlier; you can always roll on the throttle more. If you enter a turn too fast, you have no choice but to decelerate when you should be on the gas. Next time: slow in, fast out.

Another test that defines an appropriate entry speed is whether you can safely negotiate the corner *while rolling on the throttle throughout the turn.* I'll discuss this topic in detail a bit later but for now understand that mid-corner acceleration helps stabilize the motorcycle and preserve traction. If you find yourself unable to roll on the throttle throughout the turn without decelerating, then your entry speed is likely too fast for your ability or comfort level.

THREE SPEED ADJUSTMENT FACTORS

There are three factors combined that must be balanced to achieve an appropriate entry speed:

1 Your approach speed

2 Where you begin braking

3 How hard you brake

Achieving a comfortable entry speed requires either:

- braking early with moderate brake pressure, or
- braking later with more brake pressure.

In general, it is best to brake earlier. If you inadvertently brake late, use more brake pressure to recover (without skidding). It's best to set your entry speed early enough for smooth braking and a relaxed corner entry. Get all the factors right and you will be rewarded with a higher level of safety and enjoyment.

⬊ braking for downhills

When braking for downhill corners, it's important to slow more than you would for a flat corner. This allows you to open the throttle slightly, which helps balance the weight bias between the front and rear tires for good control and traction. Depending on the steepness of the hill, achieving positive throttle can be difficult. The best solution is to slow well before the turn to a speed that is slow enough to allow you to crack the throttle slightly.

look through the turn

The "look" action actually happens throughout the whole cornering sequence.
Using your eyes to aid in cornering can be broken down into two steps:

1 Look ahead before leaning to determine entry speed and spot hazards

2 Look through the turn to help direct the motorcycle

Visual direction control is the term used to describe how your eyes and attention help direct
your motorcycle where you want it to go. Of all the "aha" moments my students experience,
a majority of them occur upon realizing the power of visual direction control.

Continue to look toward the corner exit to identify whether the radius continues to be what
you expect and what road features are ahead. With this information you can accurately
judge when and how much to accelerate (see Cornering Drill #2).

initiate lean

Once you have set your entry speed then it's time to initiate lean. We talked earlier about how countersteering is the most efficient way to initiate lean; press the handlebar on the side toward which you want to turn. What we need to discuss next is where to initiate lean and how to establish the correct *amount* of lean to match the corner radius and cornering line of the turn you're about to enter.

The point at which you initiate lean is called the Turn-in location. Exactly where that point is depends on your cornering plan, based on a corner's characteristics. Depending on your approach speed and the corner radius, your turn-in location may be early, late, or somewhere in between. An early turn-in is appropriate for the early apex cornering line of an increasing radius corner, whereas a late turn-in is necessary for the delayed apex typical of a decreasing radius corner.

⬐ quick turn-in

A slow, gradual entry is appropriate for casual cornering, but a quick turn-in is required when speeds increase and the corners become tight and unpredictable.

A quick turn-in has other advantages:

1. The ability to go quickly from upright to leaned increases confidence and is a major factor in cornering safely if you must correct a misjudged corner entry. In contrast, a lack of counter-steering confidence and a slow or lazy turn-in can cause you to miss the entry and run wide.

2. Another benefit of turning quickly is that it puts your motorcycle at the maximum required lean angle early in the turn, which gets much of the direction change completed in a shorter amount of time and space. This results in your motorcycle being pointed toward the inside of the corner near the exit rather than toward the outside edge of the road (see Cornering Drill #6).

3. Because much of the direction change is completed early, the amount of time and distance at full lean is reduced. This allows you to stand your motorcycle up earlier and get on the throttle sooner, compared to a slow turn-in. (Read Keith Code's *Twist of the Wrist* series for more on this topic.)

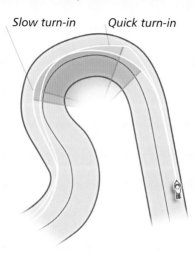

Slow turn-in   *Quick turn-in*

↘ three turning assistants

Decelerating past the turn-in point or using trail braking helps the motorcycle to turn, because the front tire is loaded, providing more traction for turning, and the forks are compressed, which quickens steering. Carefully modulate the amount of handlebar force with front brake force to prevent traction loss.

You can help initiate lean by positioning your upper body toward the inside of the motorcycle; this makes turn-in quicker and easier. I discuss body position and its effects on cornering in greater detail in Chapter 9. Also, see Body Position Drills #1, 2, and 3.

Once you have established lean angle, it is important to relax and allow your bike to track through the turn. Tension inhibits your motorcycle's inherent ability to corner and can transfer unwanted inputs to the frame and over-tax the tire's ability to hold the road. Only slight steering adjustments should be necessary to maintain a smooth line through the turn.

Your "countersteering press" may be slight or forceful; how forcefully you countersteer also depends on your cornering plan. Light countersteering is used with a relatively relaxed approach speed in combination with a gentle turn. More forceful countersteering is needed to negotiate sharp turns taken at a higher rate of speed. Aim to use one precise countersteer action to establish the correct lean rather than several actions that can upset handling.

Two factors must be coordinated to determine turn-in location:

1 Approach speed
2 How quickly you turn

To avoid running wide in a corner with a fast approach speed requires either an earlier turn-in location that allows light countersteering pressure, or a later turn-in which necessitates a quicker, more forceful turn-in.

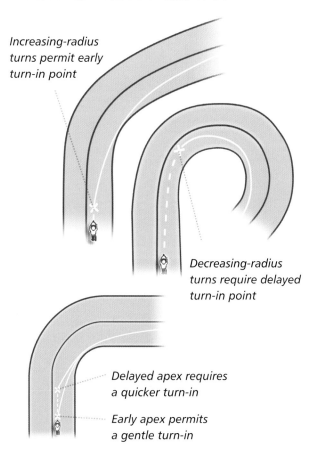

Increasing-radius turns permit early turn-in point

Decreasing-radius turns require delayed turn-in point

Delayed apex requires a quicker turn-in

Early apex permits a gentle turn-in

↘ slow-speed corners

Parking lot cornering may not seem like a maneuver worthy of discussion, but botched slow speed maneuvers can wreck your confidence and bring you a lot of embarrassment. Learning to master this often-intimidating and very challenging skill further bolsters your self-image as a proficient rider. You perform slow-speed maneuvers every ride you take, each presenting you with an opportunity to express this mastery.

What makes slow-speed handling so difficult is the lack of inertia and gyroscopic forces that keep your motorcycle stable and upright at higher speeds. The slower you go, the more unstable the bike becomes.

The procedure for performing a slow-speed turn is to:

1. Maintain *steady* drive for stability. For best control adjust speed by slipping the clutch or dragging the rear brake while holding the throttle steady.
2. Turn your head to look over your shoulder where you want to go.
3. Lean the motorcycle and turn the handlebars for balance.
4. To carve a tighter arc while remaining in balance, keep your body upright by weighting the outside footpeg, or "counterweight" with your butt off the outside of the seat.

accelerate through the turn

The final stage of cornering is rolling on the throttle. Driving force should begin just after the turn-in location and continue past the apex to the corner exit. At minimum, you want to roll on the throttle enough to maintain speed which is necessary to counteract the engine braking resistance that occurs as you lean onto the smaller diameter sides of the tires. However, you will reap the greatest benefit of corner acceleration with a bit more driving force. Use progressively more throttle application from corner entry to the exit.

Accelerating through a corner helps stabilize your motorcycle and manage traction by equalizing weight bias between front and rear tires. It also increases ground clearance by acting upon the swingarm to raise the chassis, keeping the suspension near the middle of its travel to absorb bumps and the tires in contact with the road.

Driving force can be used to adjust your turning radius and lean angle. This is useful in correcting oversteer—a bit of acceleration can widen the cornering arc just enough to push you away from the inside of the turn. Well-timed driving force straightens your motorcycle out of its lean to help the motorcycle "drift" to the outside at the corner exit and assist in making quick transitions from left-to-right and right-to-left (see Cornering Drill #4).

Acceleration stabilizes your motorcycle while cornering, but can cause problems if driving force is excessive. Avoid rear tire slides by accelerating smoothly and identifying areas of reduced traction. To precisely modulate extreme driving force when exiting corners racers will imagine the throttle mechanism as a ratchet, using each "click" as a measure to help avoid applying too much acceleration, too soon.

Throttle timing is important for optimum cornering control. Remember that acceleration decreases front tire load and traction. By delaying throttle until just after turn-in, you keep the suspension compressed and weight on the front tire for a sharper steering response. Delaying acceleration in combination with trail braking produces the most responsive steering.

That said, waiting *too* long to begin corner acceleration can result in instability. Mid-corner deceleration asks more of the front tire and tends to make the motorcycle reluctant to hold a precise line. One reason many people delay throttle roll-on is that they enter turns too fast. To avoid the effects of delayed acceleration and throttle-induced instability, slow early so you can roll on the throttle smoothly as soon as you tip your motorcycle into the turn. Roll on the throttle gradually for maximum control.

cornering problems

If you enter a turn too fast, the best thing to do is continue to look through the turn and lean more. If your entry is extremely overspeed, where more lean would present ground clearance or tire adhesion problems, then it's best to straighten the bike, brake to scrub off speed, then get back into the lean as quickly as possible. This is a tricky maneuver and should be considered a last ditch effort to save yourself from a lowside crash. Of course, this is only possible if you have enough room to straighten the bike without going off the road or into oncoming traffic. If straightening is not possible, then decelerate and brake *gently* as you maintain lean angle to stay in your lane.

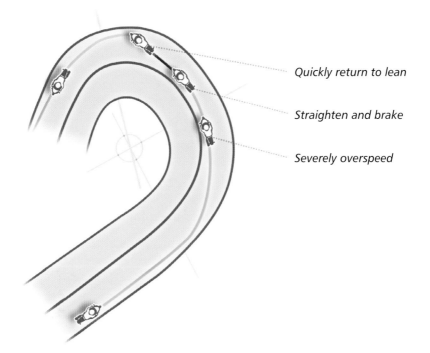

Quickly return to lean

Straighten and brake

Severely overspeed

↘ on your next ride

Every time you corner, practice rolling on the throttle as smoothly as you can throughout the duration of the corner without decelerating. Roll on the throttle so the engine pulls you all the way through to the corner exit. Reduce entry speed more than you normally do if this seems too challenging. Steady, controlled acceleration rewards you with more cornering control and confidence (see Cornering Drills #3 and #4).

cornering practice

Cornering practice will solidify your understanding of cornering dynamics and make proper cornering technique an integral part of your everyday riding. With this knowledge and experience you will be able to control your motorcycle masterfully, which increases confidence and safety.

cornering drills

PARKING LOT SETUP
You'll need an area approximately 150 feet long to weave back and forth from a straight line and an area that will allow you to ride a circle approximately 100 feet in diameter.

For these drills it is very important that you choose appropriate speeds. Remember that pushing too hard may actually set you back. These drills will demonstrate the techniques just as effectively at slower speeds as at higher speeds, so choose a conservative pace for safety. To minimize the risk of injury, wear full protective gear whenever you ride.

Press on right handlebar

cornering drill #1 - countersteering

BENEFITS

* Increase cornering confidence and "feel"
* Solidify your understanding of how to initiate lean

Press on left handlebar

INSTRUCTIONS

* Weave left and right by using handlebar pressure only.
* Press forward on the handlebar on the side toward which you want to turn; press right to go right, press left to go left.
* With each weave increase handlebar pressure and maintain pressure longer to make larger turns.

Press on right handlebar

* Consciously lighten your grip on the outside handlebar as you press forward on the inside grip to prevent unwanted counter-resistance.
* Keep your arms relaxed and bent at the elbows.

Press on left handlebar

* After some time, pull on the outside handlebar while pushing on the inside handlebar for added effect.
* Notice that the more forcefully you push/pull, the quicker your motorcycle responds.

Press on right handlebar

* Notice that the longer you hold the forward pressure, the more your motorcycle leans.

cornering drill #2 - look

BENEFITS

- ◆ Train your eyes to scan well ahead in corners to see potential hazards early
- ◆ Learn to guide your motorcycle on your intended path using visual direction control (see pages 56 and 108)

INSTRUCTIONS

1. Ride four revolutions of the circle to the left. Monitor nearby surface hazards as needed, but focus most of your visual attention well ahead, across the circle.
2. Keep your throttle steady and arms relaxed.
3. Repeat to the right.

cornering drill #3 - corner entry speed

GOAL

To adjust corner entry speed smoothly and accurately

BENEFITS

* Increase cornering judgement and safety
* Increase control by adjusting entry speed accurately to allow steady throttle throughout the curve
* Increase your ability to transition smoothly between braking and leaning (see page 82)

INSTRUCTIONS

1. Approach the right edge of the circle at 30 mph to make a left hand turn.
2. Slow to an appropriate entry speed using both brakes.
3. Enter the turn by releasing the brakes and pressing on the inside handlebar.
4. Ride the circle while gradually increasing speed and lean angle.
5. Look through the center of the circle.
6. Exit the curve. Repeat to the right.

cornering drill #4 - throttle control

BENEFITS

- ◆ Maintain steady throttle throughout the curve and to use throttle to alter the path
- ◆ Understand how the throttle affects cornering

SETUP

A circle at least 100 feet in diameter

INSTRUCTIONS

PART 1

1 Ride the circle to the left in second gear.

2 Maintain steady throttle.

3 Relax your arms and keep your wrist down
to help the throttle remain stable over bumps.

4 Exit the curve by accelerating to help straighten the bike.

5 Repeat to the right.

PART 2

Same as above, but use slight, smooth throttle adjustments
to experience how the throttle affects cornering line.

- ◆ Roll on the throttle to widen the line.
- ◆ Rolling off slightly will tighten your line. Avoid abrupt deceleration.
- ◆ Exit the curve by accelerating to help straighten the bike.
- ◆ Repeat to the right.

Maintain steady handlebar pressure and relax your arms to feel the effect.

cornering drill #5 - lean

BENEFITS

- Increase comfort with greater lean angles and cornering confidence
- Increase your ability to lean further when necessary
- Refine control at more extreme lean angles

SETUP

100 foot circle

INSTRUCTIONS

1 Ride four revolutions of the circle to the left.

2 Gradually increase speed and lean angle.
   If you prefer less speed, reduce the circle radius.

3 Keep your eyes and your attention on the circle's center.

4 Keep your throttle steady and arms relaxed.

5 Repeat to the right.

cornering drill #6 - quick turn-in

BENEFITS

- ◆ Increase cornering confidence by developing your ability to turn quickly (see page 109)
- ◆ Increase turning precision
- ◆ Expand cornering line options

INSTRUCTIONS

1 Accelerate slowly toward the right edge of the circle to make a left hand turn.

2 Delay turn-in, keeping your eyes straight ahead until just before turning.

3 Turn quickly by pressing firmly on the inside handlebar. Do not jab the handlebar too aggressively.

4 Roll on the throttle as you ride around the circle and exit.

5 Keep your eyes and your attention on the circle's center.

6 Repeat to the right.

9

Body position and posture significantly affect comfort and control. Comfortable ergonomics will help you stay fully focused on the tasks at hand. If your shoulders or butt start to complain partway through a ride, it will be difficult to concentrate.

Proper body positioning can also increase your sensitivity to feedback, aid steering, and help manage traction. How you position yourself on your motorcycle also influences the quality of interaction between you and your motorcycle. A skilled dancer positions his body perfectly for maximum balance and grace. His partner responds in kind and the two move elegantly through space. Imagine yourself as the dancer and your motorcycle as your partner; with knowledge and practice, you have the potential to ride with the same balance of elegance and grace. The ability to move as one with your motorcycle in this way brings great satisfaction.

posture

hands

Your hands play a major role in handling your motorcycle. For optimum comfort and control take the time to adjust the motorcycle's controls. A rule of thumb for adjusting brake and clutch levers is to position them so your wrists are flat when your hands squeeze the levers.

Throttle management is critical for safe, skillful riding. The amount of wrist movement needed for precise throttle control is typically quite small. To limit wrist movement, position your wrist slightly below your knuckles. For additional control, you can anchor your thumb or forefinger on the handlebar control pod, which can be helpful when doing slow maneuvers.

A wrist-down position aids throttle control.

feet and legs

Your feet are used for gear shifting and rear wheel braking, but it may not be immediately obvious just how significant your feet and legs are in unifying your body to your motorcycle's chassis. To demonstrate how much your legs affect stability, try dangling them off each side of your bike while riding at slow speeds; your bike will undoubtedly feel a bit wobbly.

Most motorcyclists habitually position the arches of their feet on the footpegs, which is fine for most situations. But, positioning the *balls* of your feet on the pegs has certain advantages, including keeping your feet from dragging on the ground at full lean and making it easier to reposition your torso for hanging off and modulating footpeg pressure. If your bike has floorboards, you can position your feet on the back edge of the floorboards.

Your feet and legs are also useful to help your motorcycle's suspension remain at its optimum compression. Supporting more of your body weight on your footpegs when riding over bumps allows your legs to become another suspension component. This is especially helpful when negotiating bumpy corners and crossing obstacles such as railroad tracks.

Keep the balls of your feet on the pegs to prevent dragging and to aid in modulating footpeg pressure.

torso and arms

It is most important to position your upper torso correctly. Shoulder and hip positions are particularly important because of the relatively high leverage your torso has on the motorcycle's center of gravity.

Because your arms and shoulders have a direct effect on handling, it is important to relax your upper torso. Keep your elbows slightly bent to allow the handlebars to turn without rotating your shoulders. Isolating your upper body mass from the handlebars allows the motorcycle to maneuver more fluidly.

Your motorcycle will carve a consistent corner radius if it can respond to surface irregularities with fluid suspension action. Stiff arms restrict handlebar movements and hinder the motorcycle's natural self-correcting actions. If you hold the handlebars too tightly, bumps are not as easily absorbed by the front suspension, which can cause your tire to slide.

You can test whether your body position and muscle tone is conducive to upper torso relaxation by sitting on your bike, then letting go of the handlebars. Notice that your leg and abdominal muscles keep your position stationary and allow your arms to be relaxed. Now put your hands on the handlebars. If you cannot "flap" your elbows easily, your upper body is too tense and you lack support from the core muscles of your abdomen and legs.

Changes in body position are useful for more than cornering. For instance, a forward position above the gas tank while accelerating over a hill will help prevent an unwanted wheelie. A rearward position when surmounting an obstacle will shift weight off the front wheel, allowing the suspension to extend and absorb the impact of the obstacle. When braking, keep a neutral position with bent elbows by squeezing the gas tank with your knees for support.

Bent elbows and relaxed arms help your motorcycle respond to surface irregularities and allows the tires to grip the road.

Stiff arms inhibit steering and can lead to a lack of cornering confidence.

feedback

Proper body position that permits a light grip on the handlebars not only contributes to your comfort and control, it also allows you to sense subtle feedback coming from your motorcycle's suspension and tires. This feedback may manifest as steering resistance or as vibration felt at the handle grips. It is here where the nerves in your hands sense how well your suspension is working or whether there is sufficient traction for control. Things to feel for are variations in handlebar resistance and changes in vibration level and frequency. To realize the full potential of your motorcycle and its tires you must learn to grip the handlebars firmly but gently, because tension mutes these sensations.

don't fight it

Riding a motorcycle well requires you to understand clearly what inputs are needed for optimum control. If you continually feel like you must force your motorcycle to do your will, you may not be giving the motorcycle the correct inputs. Most modern motorcycles are very well balanced and very responsive; it is the rider's job simply to initiate lean, then relax to limit unnecessary inputs that can upset handling.

↘ gloves and boots for feedback

To better feel the subtle sensations coming from their machines, racers fit relatively hard handlebar grips, thinly padded seats, and rigid footpegs to their motorcycles. Hard boot soles and thin, durable material covering their palms allow this information to reach the nerves in the rider's feet and hands unimpeded.

body steering

Countersteering is the most effective way to initiate lean, but body positioning also plays a role in assisting the turning process. The effects of body steering can be felt by simply moving your head and shoulders off-center, toward the inside of a turn. Positioning your upper body in this way initiates a slight change in direction. Additionally, there is a natural tendency for your inside arm to press on the inside handlebar to aid counter-steering. This combination is effective at helping to initiate lean.

Positioning your body before initiating lean assists the quick turn-in technique. When you move your body off-center the motorcycle begins to turn. To keep the motorcycle running in a straight line and prevent it from turning prematurely you'll need to hold pressure on the outside bar. When you're ready to turn, release pressure on the outside handlebar and countersteer into the corner. The result is a rapid turn-in. (See Lee Parks' book *Total Control* for more on this subject.)

Your legs and feet can also affect cornering. For instance, a firm press into the fuel tank with your outside thigh can be effective at tightening a cornering line. This is a useful technique when any additional handlebar inputs could overtax front tire grip. Depending on the size of your motorcycle and the speed you're going the result may be quite evident or quite subtle.

↘ on your next ride

Take some time to determine whether you might be struggling with your motorcycle. Try to detect upper body tension and observe whether you are giving your bike mixed messages. For instance, notice if you are pressing on both handlebars when countersteering or positioning your body in a way that resists fluid cornering.

Recognize these problems and learn to give your bike the proper inputs. Over time, your awareness will expand and you'll be able to identify and eliminate this tension. The result will be an economy of energy and a natural, fluid interaction between you and your motorcycle.

hanging off

More dramatic effects occur when you combine upper and lower body positioning into the "hang off" posture. The hanging off technique is used mostly by racers, but street riders—particularly cruiser riders—can also benefit from hanging off as a way to preserve mid-corner ground clearance. Moving the mass of the rider inside means the motorcycle doesn't have to lean as much for a given speed and turn radius. This also helps reduce steering effort.

body position drills

Described below are three hang off techniques, each useful for different situations. The hang off technique may be disorienting at first, but you can learn it with a little practice .

PARKING LOT SETUP
You'll need an area that will allow you to ride a circle approximately 100 feet in diameter (about 10 parking spaces).

body position drill #1 - basic hang off

The basic technique is useful in most situations as a way to gently influence turning effort and increase ground clearance.

BENEFITS

- Ease cornering effort
- Increase cornering confidence
- Increase leaning precision
- Increase connection with your motorcycle

INSTRUCTIONS

1 Ride around the circle to the left. Position your shoulders off-center toward the inside of the turn and perpendicular to the motorcycle with your chin over your inside elbow or forearm. Initiate lean by countersteering.

2 Look through the curve.

3 Relax your arms.

4 Repeat to the right.

Notice how an inside body position affects cornering.

body position drill #2 - intermediate hang off

The intermediate technique adds more body steering into the equation and is useful when cornering more aggressively.

Rock your hips so your body weight is on your inside butt cheek. Your shoulders and upper body will naturally move inside of your motorcycle's centerline when you rock your hips. (Try it now while sitting in your chair.) Bend at the waist so your outside shoulder is over the gas tank centerline.

Rock your hips just enough to cause the motorcycle to follow the corner path. Gentle corners respond well to slight inside weight shifts, whereas tighter, faster corners need more weight shifts. This can be thought of as "steering from the seat."

BENEFITS
- ◆ Decrease cornering effort compared to Basic Hang Off
- ◆ Increase cornering confidence
- ◆ Increase leaning precision
- ◆ Increase cornering clearance
- ◆ Increase connection with your motorcycle

BEFORE THE TURN
1 Position your butt slightly to the inside of your motorcycle's centerline by simply rocking your hips to the left for left-hand turns, and right for right-hand turns and weighting your inside butt bone.
2 Shoulders and chin should naturally follow your hips to the inside as described in the Basic Hang Off drill. Initiate lean by countersteering.

IN THE TURN
- ◆ Ride around the circle to the left in second gear.
- ◆ Look through the curve.
- ◆ Relax your arms.
- ◆ Repeat to the right.

Notice how an exaggerated body position affects cornering.

body position drill #3 - the full hang off position

The full hang off technique is used mostly for high-performance riding typically done on racetracks. Riders on cruiser-style motorcycles can use the full hang off technique to keep hard parts from dragging.

Well before entering the curve, place one full butt cheek off the inside of the seat. Use your legs to lift and sit rather than slide. Position your shoulders off-center toward the inside of the turn and perpendicular to the motorcycle with your chin over your inside forearm.

BENEFITS

- ◆ Further decrease cornering effort compared to Intermediate Hang Off
- ◆ Increase cornering confidence
- ◆ Increase leaning precision
- ◆ Increase cornering clearance
- ◆ Increase connection with your motorcycle

BEFORE THE TURN

1 Position the ball of your inside foot on the foot peg.

2 Position one full butt cheek off the edge of the seat; lift and sit rather than slide.

3 Shoulders and chin should naturally follow your hips to the inside as described for the Intermediate Hang Off. Initiate lean by countersteering.

4 Your inside leg can be kept close to the bike or extended in position as though to drag a knee.

IN THE TURN

- ◆ Ride around the circle to the left in second gear.
- ◆ Look through the curve.
- ◆ Relax your arms.
- ◆ Repeat to the right.

Notice how a more extreme inside body position affects cornering.

↘ knee dragging

Knee dragging looks cool, but it takes extreme lean angles to get a knee down—lean angles you should not attempt on public roads. Racers touch knee sliders to the tarmac primarily as a lean-angle gauge to indicate whether they have more lean angle available and whether they are on a "hot" lap (or not) by noting exactly where their knee touches down and how long they drag their knee through a corner.

hang off refinement

1 To minimize unwanted instability from late body positioning and to quicken turn-in, position your body well before the turn-in point, typically before or during braking.

2 Position the balls of your feet on the footpegs for maximum ground clearance.

3 Position yourself for maximum relaxation. Find a position on the seat that allows firm contact between your legs and the gas tank so your arms can be relaxed with a light grip on the handlebars.

4 Keep your inside shoulder and chin low and over your inside elbow or forearm. This can help prevent a "crossed up" posture where your butt is hanging off, but your shoulders and head are still centered over the bike.

5 Resist hanging off more than necessary. It may look cool, but adds little benefit and will contribute to fatigue.

You can use the first two techniques to build confidence before you attempt the full hang off technique. Get comfortable with the basic technique, then move to the intermediate technique and finally put it all together into the full hang off technique.

Maximize the communication between you and your motorcycle by paying attention to how body tension and position affect your bike and influence handling and control. Active body positioning allows you to interact harmoniously with your motorcycle and the road and contributes significantly to riding confidence while increasing the probability of zone experiences.

10

Shifting gears may not seem like an act that warrants much discussion. But, poorly timed clutch, gearshift, and throttle actions can lead to jerky gear changes that disrupt concentration and undermine your sense of masterful control. Moreover, uncoordinated downshifting technique can even lead to traction loss. In contrast, masterful shifting technique allows you to experience the joy of seamlessly accelerating up through the gears and performing almost undetectable transitions when downshifting.

A typical ride involves dozens if not hundreds of gearshifts. Learning to shift correctly takes practice, but after a while this skill becomes ingrained into your muscles and the more instinctive this ability, the less attention is spent focusing on simply getting from one gear to another.

The primary reason for shifting from one gear to another is to match the engine speed (RPM) with the road speed and to keep the engine in its usable power range. This means upshifting when speeding up and downshifting when slowing down or when more power is needed. In this chapter, you'll learn the nuances of downshifting and upshifting, including techniques that can make shifting smoother.

⬎ clutchwork

We usually don't think of the clutch as anything more than a device that allows us to get underway and shift gears, but the clutch is also an important control to achieve smooth power delivery. To fine-tune speed adjustments you can minimize lurching by "slipping" the clutch in the engagement zone rather than using the often-touchy throttle. This is most useful when riding slowly.

Developing fine clutch control begins with knowing exactly where in the lever's range of travel disengagement and reengagement occurs. Knowing when the clutch will engage allows you to control engine braking when downshifting. Also, matching precise clutch engagement with an appropriate amount of throttle allows you to start skillfully from a stop on uphills.

downshifting

Downshifting to a lower gear is done to match the engine speed to a slower road speed or for getting the engine to rev higher for more power. Many riders also use downshifting as a way to slow the motorcycle. Using engine braking for minor speed adjustments usually causes no control problems. However, using engine braking for significant speed reduction can result in abrupt deceleration or loss of rear tire traction if you don't release the clutch carefully.

Downshifting must be performed smoothly to avoid instability and possible loss of control that can occur from forcing the rear tire to abruptly change speed to match engine RPM. Poor timing and abrupt clutch engagement can cause your motorcycle to lurch and your rear wheel to skid briefly. You can hear the results of poor downshifting by the "chirping" sound made by the tire as it skids momentarily on the pavement.

To avoid rough downshifts it's important to ease out the clutch lever slowly to allow the engine RPMs to rise gradually. To prevent excessive engine braking delay downshifts until the engine RPMs are relatively low. Also try to keep engine RPMs from falling to idle during downshifting by rolling off the throttle *partially*. This way the engine revs don't have far to climb to match the lower gear ratio.

Because of the possibility of excessive engine braking and the resultant loss of traction it's best to avoid downshifting while cornering. If you must downshift mid-corner, do so gently.

throttle blipping

The easiest way to prevent jarring downshifts is to simply ease the clutch out slowly, but some riders prefer the "throttle blip" technique. Throttle blipping is performed by quickly twisting the throttle on and off for a fraction of a second while the clutch is squeezed during the downshift. The objective is to get engine RPM matched to the lower gear ratio before releasing the clutch.

Done properly, the whole throttle blipping downshift occurs in less than a second. It's important to squeeze the clutch quickly while simultaneously downshifting the transmission and blipping the throttle with your right hand. This is repeated with every downshift, one gear at a time.

shifting up

To upshift squeeze the clutch, shift into the next gear, and release the clutch to smoothly reengage power. To prevent lurching strive for well-timed throttle, clutch, and gearshift actions that lead to smooth upshifting.

quick upshift

Some riders shift slowly and deliberately. However, leisurely upshifts can result in jerky power transitions as the engine RPMs drop too low to match the road speed when you release the clutch. To minimize rough upshifts caused by excessive RPM drops, keep the throttle open slightly as you perform the shift and shift quickly.

Whether shifting slowly or quickly, the important point is to shift in a way that minimizes driveline jerkiness. The goal is to keep a steady load on the drive train and maintain your rhythm.

�‌↘ clutchless upshifts

Clutchless upshifts are common among high performance street riders and roadracers who are interested in an even quicker shifting technique with the least power interruption. Clutchless upshifts are most appropriate for full- or nearly-full-throttle acceleration when engine RPMs are high.

Clutchless shifting requires the same steps as the quick upshift technique described earlier, but without using the clutch. At the instant you close the throttle, you shift the transmission to the next higher gear. The gear shifts at the moment the gear-box and chain go slack. Then you open the throttle instantaneously and forward drive is maintained. With good technique, the transmission experiences no additional wear.

shifting practice drills

Practicing shifting in a parking lot can familiarize you with the basic techniques discussed in this chapter. Strive for smooth upshifting and downshifting transitions. Not only will this improve control, it will also lead to a more graceful interaction between you and your motorcycle.

shifting drill #1 - quick shift

BENEFITS

- Master smooth transitions between gears
- Reduce motorcycle pitch and load transfer when shifting

INSTRUCTIONS

Accelerate, then, to shift to the next higher gear:

1. Apply light pressure to the underside of the shift lever.
2. Roll off the throttle only about 30 to 50 percent.
3. Squeeze the clutch lever about 30 to 50 percent.
4. Swiftly click the gear shift lever up.

Release the clutch lever smoothly, yet rapidly as you roll on the throttle. Done correctly, the whole process should take less than one second. Notice how a quick upshift smooths shifting by minimizing the transition time between gears.

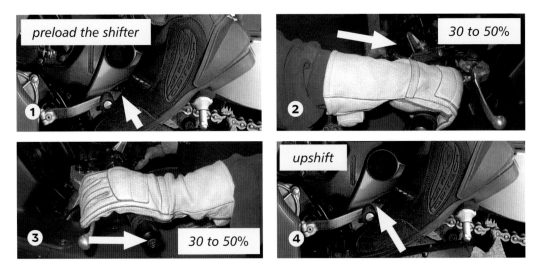

shifting drill #2 - double downshift

This downshifting drill will allow you to practice matching engine speed to road speed. To perform this drill you roll off the throttle to reduce speed, and then downshift *twice* before reengaging the clutch. Downshifting twice introduces an extreme difference in engine speed compared to the road speed, requiring careful timing and modulation of clutch release. Delay releasing the clutch until speed is reduced to avoid over-revving the engine and be sure to ease the clutch out slowly to prevent a rear tire skid.

BENEFITS

- Ease load transfer when downshifting
- Prevent rear tire skids and loss of control when downshifting

INSTRUCTIONS

1. Ride in a straight line in third gear.
2. Roll off the throttle to reduce speed.
3. Squeeze the clutch and downshift **twice.**
4. **Slowly** ease out the clutch to avoid locking the rear wheel.
   Delay clutch release to avoid overreving the motor.

A visceral connection develops between you and your motorcycle when you can smoothly click through the gears. This interaction is felt with every upshift and downshift you make. Eventually, shifting ability becomes so ingrained that you put little thought or mental energy into the task. With less attention spent focused on the mechanical execution of changing gears you have more capacity to enjoy the nuances of the riding environment and the sensations of motorcycle control.

11

You experience the deepest sense of mastery when your mind and body work together. This means that your attention is fully involved with the task of riding well and your body responds effortlessly with precise inputs that express your most subtle intent; you understand what your bike is telling you and your motorcycle's controls become extensions of your fingers, arms, and legs. To reach this level of mastery requires ongoing education and practice.

The techniques discussed within this book are intended to help you achieve a mastery of motorcycle riding. To make these techniques a permanent part of your skillset takes continual practice over weeks, months, and years.

Purposeful practice can help new riders cross the threshold from beginner to intermediate and veteran riders to improve their survival and control skills. Whatever your experience level, keep your riding challenging and enjoyable by seeking out opportunities to learn and grow.

When working on skills, start slowly, learning new techniques at a rate you can absorb. Being overwhelmed can easily result in hampered growth and possibly a panic-induced crash, neither of which lead you to a greater sense of confidence.

stay sharp

There are two basic ways to learn: you can learn by experiences that "happen" to you, or you can "seek out" learning opportunities. The former puts you in the role of victim; the latter puts you in control.

Seek out *skilled* riders (not merely *experienced* riders) for their advice. Enroll in riding courses and read books and articles about riding techniques, then practice what you learned. The idea is to develop your skills *before* you need them. Practice doesn't have to be formal. You can practice on every ride you take; opportunities to refine braking and cornering control abound. Take information you've read or heard and give it a try.

Even though practice can be informal and impromptu, it's best to be *purposeful* about it. Be fully aware that you are trying something new and evaluate whether it has a positive or negative effect.

Remember that in motorcycling, mental skills are just as important as physical skills. Use what you've learned in this book to develop and practice traffic strategies; consciously apply them to your riding (and driving) to make them habitual.

parking lot practice

Sometimes the street is not the best place to practice. For developing new physical skills at a safe speed and in a controlled environment there is no better place than an empty, clean parking lot.

Before you discount parking lot practice as irrelevant to actual street riding, I can tell you as a veteran motorcycle safety instructor that parking lot practice is indeed relevant. Motorcyclists who learn to negotiate a tight parking lot circuit lined with little orange cones become much more confident at both low and high-speed control on the street.

USE CAUTION AND COMMON SENSE

At the end of each chapter are parking lot drills designed to help you learn and master many of the techniques discussed in this book. Please use common sense in setting up these drills. Choose an area that is clear of debris and other traction-compromising conditions.

It is also very important that you choose appropriate speeds. Remember that pushing too hard will often set you back, not move you forward. These drills will demonstrate the concepts just as effectively at slower speeds than at higher speeds, so choose a conservative pace for safety. To minimize the risk of injury, wear full protective gear whenever you ride.

street practice

Parking lot practice is great, but you'll want to put these techniques into service on the street as soon as possible. Each and every ride you take is an opportunity to expand your traffic strategies and improve your control skills. Look for the "On Your Next Ride" sidebars for suggestions of specific things to try on any ride. Try these skills every chance you get to develop your skills more rapidly and have more fun.

The techniques described in this book are appropriate for the street, but be conscious that the street has many unpredictable variables compared to a parking lot; therefore you must carefully choose when and where to stretch your limits.

track days

The absolute best place to develop and re-fine advanced braking and cornering techniques is on the racetrack. Before you turn the page thinking that a track day isn't for you, listen up.

It's important to understand that track days are not race events! It's understandable that people assume track days mean racing, after all track days happen on a racetrack. Not that many years ago you *would* have had to mount a number plate and get a competition license just to turn a wheel on a racetrack. But, these days that's not true. Track days are offered at many racetracks across the world to provide typical street riders with an opportunity to ride their motorcycle in an environment unencumbered by oncoming traffic, turning vehicles, unexpected surface hazards, animals, pedestrians, and police.

Track days and track schools are a great way for any rider on almost any type of bike to develop their skills without the typical dangers of street riding. And, where else can you revisit several corners multiple times in a single day to perfect your technique? Many track day organizations have instructors available to help you get the most out of your day. Ask one or two instructors to follow you around and to give you an honest appraisal of where you need to focus your skill-building efforts.

I encourage you to bring this book to a track day and practice some of the techniques described. You will come away with a smile on your face and a more intimate relationship with your motorcycle and riding.

the road ahead

I hope I've convinced you that you can increase your level of safety, enjoyment, and riding confidence by increasing your knowledge and skill. I also hope that the information and drills in this book and video assists in your goal to become a better and safer rider. To keep these techniques fresh in your mind reread this book periodically and watch the video over and over. And don't skimp on practice time. Train your mind and body to respond correctly and you'll surely increase confidence and the probability of many zone experiences.

acknowledgements

The ideas and techniques outlined in this book are derived from my personal campaign to become the best rider I can be, with the goal of enjoying riding to the fullest. My thirst for higher learning was stimulated by the likes of David L. Hough, Keith Code, Lee Parks, Nick Ienatsch, and Reg Pridmore, as well as many others who chose to share their knowledge through books and magazines. I thank all these people for making motorcycling safer and more enjoyable.

A book like this is possible only with a lot of support. I thank my wife, Caroline, and daughter, Jeannine for putting up with me as I tapped away at the keyboard for hours on end and for giving their input when asked. Also, thanks to my dad for introducing me to motorcycles and my mom for allowing it.

I also want to recognize Dan Kennedy of Whitehorse Press for his support and belief in this project. And thanks to Dave Searle for trusting me with *Motorcycle Consumer News'* Proficient Motorcycling column for these past several years, and former MCN editor, Fred Rau for his support. Above all I must direct my greatest appreciation toward my personal mentor, David Hough, who spent countless hours turning this motorcycle enthusiast into an author. Without Mr. Hough none of this would have been possible.

The author with daughter Jeannine and wife Caroline take a break at Deal's Gap, 2002.

David Hough shows me the fine points of sidecar touring, 2003.

index

use of the accompanying dvd

The DVD packaged with this book is double-sided (DVD-10 format). One side of the DVD is recorded in NTSC video, with PAL on the other side. The NTSC analog television system is used in North America, Japan, and other parts of the world. The PAL system is used in Europe, Australia, India, and other parts of the world. To play the DVD using the NTSC standard, insert the DVD into the player with the NTSC label facing up; use the opposite side for the PAL standard.